Notes
Fireground

Notes from the Fireground

Memoir of a
New York Firefighter

THOMAS DUNNE

McFarland & Company, Inc., Publishers
Jefferson, North Carolina

Library of Congress Cataloguing-in-Publication Data

Names: Dunne, Thomas, 1950– author.
Title: Notes from the fireground : memoir of a New York firefighter /
    Thomas Dunne.
Description: Jefferson, North Carolina : McFarland & Company, Inc.,
    Publishers, 2020 | Includes index.
Identifiers: LCCN 2020002122 | ISBN 9781476679884 (paperback :
    acid free paper) ∞
    ISBN 9781476638706 (ebook)
Subjects: LCSH: Dunne, Thomas, 1950- | New York (N.Y.). Fire Department. |
    Fire fighters—New York (State)—New York—Biography.
Classification: LCC TH9118.D86 A3 2020 | DDC 363.37092 [B]—dc23
LC record available at https://lccn.loc.gov/2020002122

British Library cataloguing data are available

ISBN (print) 978-1-4766-7988-4
ISBN (ebook) 978-1-4766-3870-6

Front cover photograph © 2020 Shutterstock

Printed in the United States of America

McFarland & Company, Inc., Publishers
    Box 611, Jefferson, North Carolina 28640
    www.mcfarlandpub.com

To my father, Francis Dunne, who started it all.
To Suzanne, Kevin, Erica, and Tatiana. And to the
many firefighters who weren't as lucky as me.

The fire which enlightens is the same fire which consumes.—Henri Frederic Amiel

Table of Contents

Acknowledgments

My sincere thanks to the many firefighters I had the pleasure to meet over the 33 years I spent with the New York City Fire Department. You are an amazing group of people. It was an honor to work with you and to be a part of the FDNY.

A special note of gratitude to Dennis Smith and all of the other old breed firefighters who worked during the "war years" of the FDNY when New York City was burning every night. You set the standard for generations of firefighters.

Thanks also to the editorial staff at McFarland for taking on this project and to the photographers who graciously shared their work.

To my family, my appreciation for the warmth and support you always provide. Kevin and Erica, I am so proud of the people you are. And to my wife, the novelist Suzanne Chazin, thanks for the guidance and example you set. You are the only real writer in the family.

Author's Note

All of the events depicted in this book actually occurred, and all of the people are real. I have changed the names of most of them in order to protect their privacy.

Preface

I was truly shot. Mentally and physically. It was about a week after the September 11 attack and I was standing at a command post supervising a sector of the World Trade Center recovery operation. The day was going just like all the previous ones had: long, draining, and surreal. It had only been a week but it felt like I had been there much longer, like time had stopped altogether and those acres of devastation were going to replace and overwhelm any remnant of my previous life. Even the exquisite Indian summer weather that surrounded me seemed irrelevant. By now the initial shock of the attack had been transformed into an endless daily grind of literally and figuratively picking up the pieces of unimaginable destruction. Enormous fields of dust and twisted metal debris had replaced any semblance of what had once been an iconic workplace for thousands, many of whom lay entombed below. There was fire still burning deep within those layers of ruin and it spewed out a toxic smoke which mixed with the general stench of rotting flesh and pulverized building materials and blended with the diesel fumes that belched out of the heavy equipment maneuvering on top of it all.

The noise added to the assault. Clumps of metal crashed and shattered as the grapplers dug their way down into the steel labyrinth. A steady line of dump trucks lined the side streets, their engines roaring as they waited their turn in the endless task of slowly removing the debris load by painful load. And each of those loads created additional clouds of dust as the bent steel beams crashed loudly into the truck beds. In the background a constant barrage of urgent messages spewed from the fireground radios. Another body had been located, a hose line had to be repositioned, a worker had been injured and required medical attention. The problems were nonstop and sapped the strength of all. After several hours of this I was operating on fumes myself.

When I got hit by the harsh tobacco odor from a cigar someone was smoking nearby I had about reached my limit. On top of everything else I

1

had to deal with the stench of someone's smoking habit? I felt like screaming or just going home to get away from it all. But I couldn't do either so I
found a place to sit down and take a load off for a minute.

Someone walked by the command post carrying a bag of hamburgers. I hadn't eaten for hours and suddenly realized that I was ravenous.
Normally I didn't really like hamburgers but the person handed me one
and I started munching on it in a kind of detached mindset. It felt good
to sit in the warm September sun for a few minutes, just eating and enjoying a quick respite from the relentless challenges and the disturbing
background. As I sat I noticed that there was a red plastic bag lying next
to me. It had a biohazard symbol on it indicating that it contained body
parts but I didn't need to see that to know what was inside. The smell
alone gave evidence to the bag's contents. Maybe it was the exhaustion,
or perhaps it was the constant and overwhelming presence of death and
tragedy that made me oblivious, but I just continued to eat like I was comfortably seated in a restaurant rather than immersed in a mass graveyard.
I remember thinking this wasn't normal, how could I do this? Why doesn't
this bother me?

Like most people I am sure that I have been shaped and influenced
by my chosen line of work. On the most basic level any job is a financial
arrangement that provides a monetary reward for an investment of your
time. However, for the majority of us it represents far more than that. Engaging in any type of employment for a prolonged period leaves a wealth
of memories, experiences, and impressions. Soldiers, politicians, school-
teachers, and plumbers all have their own unique work and life perspectives. My 33 years with the New York City Fire Department have certainly
left me with mine. I have been blessed with an extremely diverse and lucky
career in the FDNY, a career that has presented some of the very best and
very worst moments of my life.

Ask anybody who has been a firefighter and he will likely tell you
that it was one of the most memorable experiences of his life. Whether
it is performed on a volunteer basis or for paid employment, in a large
city or a small town, the work presents a unique blend of fear, adrenaline,
elation, humor, and fulfillment. Many individual thoughts, stories, and insights emerge from this background. Little things that, in retrospect, seem
somehow significant, observations that, for better or worse, cling to and
haunt memories. Thoughts that seem worthy of recording and sharing
with others.

Over the course of my career as I moved through the ranks from
lowly new recruit, to company officer, to fire chief, I got to see New York
City from an unusual but fascinating vantage point. In glittering mid–
Manhattan high rise buildings and in squalid ghettos I saw how people

in crisis lived and survived. And how the firefighters who protected them worked, joked, and bonded. This book is an effort to share some of these insights. Although my career was in a New York setting the story is really about firefighters everywhere and about emotions that are common to all of us.

I contemplated writing this book for a long time but always found an excuse not to actually sit down and start it. The very act of writing seemed like a specialty for other people to pursue or at least an intimidating task that lacked the linear and clear-cut direction that characterized my previous work experience. I have envisioned myself in a lot of roles but author is not one of them. However, thanks to social media we live in a society that now allows almost everyone to become some version of a writer. Blogs, tweets, e-mails, articles, and essays allow for a constant sharing of information, opinions, and experiences from many different people. Writing, it seems, is no longer the exclusive domain of those with the skill and discipline to chain themselves for hours to a computer screen. I am reminded of a quote from the writer Flannery O'Connor: "Everywhere I go I'm asked if I think the university stifles writers. My opinion is that they don't stifle enough of them."

So, rather than being stifled, I have made the choice to enthusiastically throw my hat into the writer's ring. But at the same time I have done it with a certain level of doubt and caution. I have long thought writing a memoir would be a somewhat self-indulgent and egotistical exercise. What exactly have I done that was so exceptional? I have lived an ordinary life. I have not fought in a war or accomplished any great humanitarian act and neither sought nor achieved any kind of fame. Still, a long immersion in a career that provided a front row seat in a world of life-and-death struggles has left much I want to share. I've seen some great moments as well as some ugly ones.

That being said, I had three goals in mind when writing *Notes from the Fireground*: to offer an entertaining narrative, to provide a glimpse of a unique slice of life, and, perhaps more than anything, to air out the joys, pains, and demons that lurk in my memories. Maybe you can see some of your own experiences in it and relate to feelings that we all share as we journey through life.

I wish I could begin with a classic "Call me Ishmael" type of line. But such eloquence is well beyond my literary capacity. So let's just start at the beginning.

The Smoke House

My very first fire department memory is of the mayor's bald head. I remember noting how the sun reflected off of it on that beautiful October day as he addressed our group of 300 new recruits. Ed Koch was a three-term mayor in New York City and, regardless of your political persuasion, you had to kind of like his off-the-cuff, personal style. I don't remember his exact words but they were somewhere in the category of the challenge, dedication, and commitment comments that propel these events. I remember feeling kind of guilty that all the great virtues he spoke of were going right over my head while I sat with a Zen-like focus on his shining scalp.

Somewhere out in the audience my mother and father were proudly watching. I'm sure that what they were seeing was different from what I was feeling. My dad was a 30-year veteran of the New York City Fire Department and a member of the generation that grew up during the Depression and served in World War II. He was a good man who worked hard, raised three kids, and loved being in the FDNY. He was also very security conscious and viewed my new employment as a "safe" job that would provide a steady income with a minimal chance of being laid off. We felt very close to each other but that emotion, like the pride he felt that day, was not something either of us was comfortable expressing.

I was single, childless, and generally directionless. Feeling bored and unchallenged by my previous work I looked at this new job as a chance to do something unusual and exciting. I also saw it as something I would do for one year just to have the experience and then move on to something else. Lack of commitment had been a common theme in much of my employment and many of my relationships. On this day I couldn't have imagined that I was about to embark on an experience that was to last several decades, come close to killing me, and, in the process, change the essence of who I was.

The mayor was speaking at a lectern in front of a five-story brick building that served as a training tower. Over the next several weeks I would discover that it was actually fun to climb ladders to the top of this edifice and absolutely thrilling to repel back down from the roof while dangling from a rope as if descending from some Tibetan peak. What I hadn't noticed on that first day was the building behind it. "Building Number 2" was a squat two-story structure that would become a testing ground and the source of great tears and gnashing of teeth. It was referred to simply as "the smoke house."

The architecture of a building, like any piece of art, is planned to evoke a feeling to go along with its function. If it's possible for a place to just look evil the smoke house certainly qualified. It was covered with black stains from years of fires lit in its dark interior and was designed to give new trainees the experience of breathing in a smoky environment or, as it was referred to, "taking a feed." The few exterior windows were covered by heavy, black metal shutters that were always closed, hiding the building's mysterious inner core. As lowly new trainees we had much to learn from the fire academy's training cadre and a key part of our education would involve an intimate introduction to its shadowy environment.

The old, wood-burning smoke house has long since been replaced by a modern, propane-fueled training facility (photograph by the author).

The fire department is a quasi-military organization with the emphasis on the military while in the training phase and more on the quasi when actually performing the job. New recruits in the FDNY are called "probies," short for probationary firefighters. Probies are considered the absolute lowest creatures in the fire department pecking order and are treated as such. As we hustled through the initial stages of the academy the trainers continually barked orders at us, prodding and testing and demanding that we remove the lead that was apparently stuck up most of our posteriors. I loved the physical, hands-on parts of the training but despised the martial aspect of the academy. I watched in an alienated state of amazement as one of the drill instructors demonstrated the "proper" method of marching, turning, and facing about. To me he seemed ludicrous. His rigid posture contrasted entirely with the natural grace and unstructured ease I admired in the movements of agile deer and prancing horses. I was already in good physical shape and very self-disciplined and had joined the fire department for some excitement. What did all of this marching nonsense have to do with firefighting?

The training staff included a wide variety of guys. Some were sin-

The smoke-stained shutters on the new building are just as intimidating and unwelcoming as the old ones were (photograph by the author).

cerely interested in teaching new people. Others were temporarily detailed to the fire academy and were just biding their time until they could move on to better assignments. And a select evil few actually seemed to enjoy making life miserable for us.

The worst offender of those few was a senior, ancient-looking officer who was nearing the tail end of his career. He really enjoyed using intimidation as both a management and teaching tool. I on the other hand had always been somewhat of a free spirit and didn't take well to the martial aspect of the job. So this particular guy really got to me and I quickly got fed up with both him and his efforts at intimidation. One day he was addressing about 50 of us in the drill yard. For some reason we happened to make eye contact and I think that he immediately sensed that I couldn't stand him. Rather than just looking away from him and going back to my normal "invisible" status I did something I had never done before. I continued to stare at him eyeball to eyeball and tried to mentally and physically project my negative feelings about him. For no obvious reason I had drawn a mental line in the sand and wasn't going to back down in our staring war. And I won, or thought I did, because he was the one who broke eye contact and looked away. It was a small thing and probably a stupid thing but I was intent on showing that I was not going to be intimidated by him.

However, just a few hours later that same instructor was scheduled to give us a lecture in a classroom and he had obviously not forgotten me. Before the class even began he bombarded me with a series of esoteric questions about the diameters of various hose fittings. I knew I had gotten to him and now it was his revenge time. Fortunately, I had happened to read on that exact subject the night before and I gave him all the right answers. Only this time I made a point of answering respectfully, adding "sir" to my responses. I knew that I had made my first major fire department error. The main goal in probie school was to learn and get through it as anonymously as possible. For a brief moment I had stood out, and in a negative way. And shortly it would come back to haunt me.

We were not led into the smoke house for the first few days but it was always on our minds and in our discussions. When we were initially sent in it was done quickly and we were allowed to wear the face pieces of our air masks which completely protected us from breathing in the smoke. It was kind of fascinating and painless, almost like a Disneyland attraction minus the inevitably attached gift shop. That was soon to end as we were introduced to the art and agony of taking a feed.

Fires were ignited for the final exercise and the building was filled with thick smoke. Recruits then crawled in without their air masks and stayed as low as possible to avoid the dark, biting air above them. Once they were all inside a trainer would order them to stand up in the smoke and proceed to bombard them with questions, demands, and even song requests, all designed to force them to communicate and function despite the gagging conditions. This would continue for a few minutes and, just when it seemed like it would never end, a recruit stationed on the roof was ordered to open a scuttle that quickly vented out the smoke and provided immediate relief for the suffering members below.

The process was designed to reinforce two vital lessons in the most effective and tangible manner. First, you learned that you *were* able to survive a smoky condition in the event that lost your air supply in an emergency. Second, you were never going to forget the immediate relief you felt as you watched the smoke get sucked up and out of the building the moment the roof scuttle was opened. As they expressed it in the constantly reinforced training mantra, "vent and ye shall live."

Only small groups of recruits could participate in this exercise at a time and our large body of 300 trainees quickly divided into two camps: those who had been there and those who had not. I was of the group who had to wait some time to experience it. It seemed like the longer you had to wait the more threatening it appeared and the more you dreaded it. The anticipation was not helped by the stories of guys puking their guts out. One recruit who just couldn't handle it ran out of the smoke house and was immediately counseled by a trainer, "Kid, you're in the wrong fucking job." I am certain I wasn't alone in questioning if I was cut out for this line of work.

Before I actually got to experience being inside the building I was assigned to the roof position where I was responsible for opening the scuttle to vent out the smoke. That vantage point allowed for a good view of the entire training complex. The New York City Fire Academy (aka "The Rock") is located on an island in the East River. It is somewhat remote and when you travel there the limited bridge access gives it kind of a Devil's Island feel. It is bordered on one side by a railroad bridge and on the other side by a power plant that spews huge clouds of steam through several enormous chimneys. Periodically the entire area is gently perfumed by a nearby sewage plant.

From my roof vantage point I could see a scattering of training props, fire trucks, and drab buildings. Bands of new probies, whose impeccable boots and spotless gear bespoke their firefighting virginity, hustled about. And, in a final Orwellian touch, a dark window in the upper recesses of the main administrative building hovered above it all from which, we were warned, the commanding officer could observe our every move. The environment had all the physical charm and feng shui of a Russian gulag, a gritty, tough, industrial wasteland well suited as a backdrop for a harsh and unforgiving profession.

Being the scuttle man on the roof of the smoke house put me as close as possible to the activity going on below without actually being involved in it. I could hear the yelling instructors and the gagging trainees. At one point the recruits were ordered to sing Christmas carols—the image combined a scene from Charles Dickens with an episode of *Hogan's Heroes*. Witnessing it from a distance only increased my anxiety and I wished that I could jump down to join them and just get the whole thing over with.

It wasn't long before I did get my turn. Crawling in, I hugged the floor where the air was most tolerable. A cloud of dark, threatening smoke billowed just inches above. Once inside I was met by an older, red-eyed instructor who appeared in the midst of the smoke like some kind of ancient demon—the same officer I had recently confronted in eyeball to eyeball combat in the drill yard. He peered at the name on my coat and asked, "Who have we got here?" followed by a loud and triumphant exclamation of "Dunne!" and I knew that I was screwed. I was ordered to stand up and as I did, I was immediately immersed in a cloud of stinging toxins. He proceeded to "interview" me and make me speak so that I could fully appreciate the choking sensation. The unit number on his battered helmet indicated he was assigned to a busy Harlem company and he was no doubt a remnant of the era when firefighters didn't even wear masks. Despite my pain I couldn't help but notice that his leather helmet was dried out and flaking and I wondered what his lungs were like or, for that matter, what my lungs would become. He continued to test and prod my ability to handle the smoke just as he did with any other probie. Only this time he really seemed to enjoy it.

There was instant and soothing relief when the roof scuttle finally opened and the smoke vented out. Kind of what it must feel like if you finally stop hitting yourself on the head with a hammer. And, again, basic firefighting knowledge had been painfully but effectively reinforced. Just as important as the tactical lesson was the feeling that I had met with and survived a very uncomfortable experience and, as is often the case, the anticipation was much worse than the realization.

I learned a lot about smoke that day. But I also got a lesson on fear. Fear, it seems, is somewhat analogous to sex. When you are afraid you feel remarkably tantalized in anticipation of the action and pleasantly calm once it's over.

Seeing the Elephant

There was an expression used during the Civil War to describe a soldier's first experience in combat. "Seeing the elephant" may have derived from traveling circuses that roamed the country prior to the war. A trip to the circus gave farm boys an opportunity to experience exotic sights and unusual animals, visions that wildly contrasted from their predictable everyday lives. Their first view of an elephant would no doubt have been a highlight of the show and the source of an indelible memory, a memory that easily translated to describing the intense experience of being shot at for the first time.

Firefighting has been described by some as a version of combat. The danger, noise, confusion, and uncertainties are certainly characteristic of both. And a firefighter always remembers the intimate details of his first time inside a burning building.

Mine came shortly after graduating from the fire academy. I was assigned to an engine company following six weeks of basic training. Over that period I had learned to stretch and operate hose lines, slide down ropes, and climb ladders. I was also introduced to the fact that, as a new probie, I was by far the lowest entity in my new work world. As they say, the firehouse dog was ranked someplace above me in the organizational chart of the New York City Fire Department.

During the first few tours in my new unit I responded to a number of false alarms, automobile accidents, and the occasional outside rubbish fire. Sometimes I was given the "nozzle," a choice assignment that gave me an opportunity to operate the hose line and knock down flames. But I had not yet experienced a "real" incident. I had not been inside a building that was actually on fire. That was still a somewhat hazy concept to me and the thought of it kept me on the edge of my seat as I anxiously awaited finally experiencing it. I knew that I couldn't even consider myself a firefighter until I had crawled through heat and smoke and had at least helped advance a hose line to attack a room full of flames. After a number of days

I had done little more than clean the firehouse, maintain the tools, and respond to a lot of routine calls. I started to feel like the back-up quarterback on a football team who did nothing but sit on the bench, like I had been given the job description of "firefighter" but had in fact done nothing at all to earn the title.

The build-up finally ended on a December afternoon in an industrial area of the city. I was introduced to the world of interior structural firefighting at a three-story brick building that was located not far from the neighborhood I had grown up in. It had a restaurant on the first floor and two apartments above, just a typical urban building that normally blended in with the rest of its drab surroundings. In fact, I had actually driven past the place for many years and hardly even noticed it was there. However, that all changed on this day. From several blocks away I could see thick black smoke spewing from the two top floors of the building. The strange and still uncomfortable reality of my new profession kicked in as the rig came to a sudden stop at the nearest hydrant. When I was a kid growing up in Brooklyn I had been a casual observer of a number of fires that occurred in the neighborhood. This was different. I was no longer a mere observer but a participant. Now I was a firefighter (though I didn't yet feel like one) and I was experiencing excitement, fear, and confusion all at the same time.

Firefighting is an adrenaline-inducing activity even when performed by very experienced personnel. The positive side of this is that the energy surge makes you stronger and much quicker to react. And the negative side is also that it makes you stronger and much quicker to react. Without the confidence and experience to control and focus this nervous energy, it becomes much harder to concentrate and even the simplest tasks can become more difficult. With my total lifetime structural firefighting experience amounting to zero, I immediately fell prey to the dark side of excess stimulation.

The self-contained breathing apparatus (SCBA) is the most essential piece of firefighting equipment. Between basic training and daily drill periods I must have put my breathing mask on a hundred times. However, the moment I stepped onto the sidewalk and slung the mask onto my back I immediately had problems fully engaging all the belts and buckles properly. Here I was, finally arriving at my first fire, and within minutes I was a case study in frustration and embarrassment. It was at this low point that I first experienced the support and connection that even the gruffest firefighters share while working together.

Gaining acceptance in a firehouse is a slow and painful process. Most of the men in my company were senior firefighters who had worked through the "war years" of the FDNY in the late 1960s and early 1970s when sections of the Bronx and Brooklyn were burning every night. Several of them were well into their 50s, and some had beer guts, but they all carried the ethos of men who had done and seen an awful lot. As the very green new member of the unit I was able to get from them, at best, a few reluctant words of conversation. I had not shared their unique experience of running around all night and fighting numerous fires every tour they worked.

Now, here I am, the new guy, at my first structural fire and right away I am struggling. However, I quickly discovered that while I didn't bring any experience to the team, I was in fact a part of that team. The unit officer and one of the firefighters immediately stepped up to help secure my mask and then proceeded to guide me into the building. It seemed like this fire, which was such a radical new experience for me, was just a walk in the park for them. Their confidence and willingness to help allowed me to focus on the task at hand. These veterans, who previously had barely spoken to me, proceeded to guide me step by step through the first real "job" in my firefighting career.

We had arrived as the second due engine and our primary task was to assist the first unit with getting the hose line into position. Once that was accomplished we retreated to the floor below the fire to preserve the air in our masks so we could relieve the first unit when they were physically shot. I could hear all the activity going on above me. Glass was shattering, firefighters were yelling, and the officers were issuing orders that came out as muffled sounds beneath their mask face pieces. The stream from the advancing hose line added to the background noise, making a deep drumming sound as it hit the walls and ceiling. As I listened to the overload of noise above me it was hard to get any sense of order in the midst of all the chaos. Water runoff from the hose line dripped down and saturated us as we stood on the floor below. For the first time I felt that peculiar, almost sensual feeling of warm, smoky liquid dripping down my collar and neck. It would leave a scent on my body that would become quite familiar over the next three decades of my life.

By the time we were sent upstairs to relieve the unit on the hose line the fire had been largely extinguished. I was positioned on the nozzle and instructed to wash down the charred lath and plaster. As the water stream tore into and removed parts of the ceiling I discovered one of the hidden pleasures of being a firefighter. It was, quite simply, fun to destroy things. What school kid (or adult) has not fantasized about breaking glass windows, forcing doors open, or otherwise ignoring societal taboos on destroying property? Here I was not only expected to do it but I was also being paid for my efforts.

Looking back I realize that I really didn't do all that much at this, my first fire. But at the time it certainly didn't feel that way. I had been inside a burning building, overcome a number of obstacles, and actually functioned as a firefighter. Later, in the firehouse kitchen, I felt a sense of accomplishment and belonging as we sat around and discussed the operation.

In the decades following this experience I went to well over a thousand fires. After a while many of them kind of blended together and it was only the unusual ones or the ones where people died that stuck in my mind. You might think the "elephant" would have eventually disappeared, that the years of firefighting somehow dulled the intensity of the experience. But that never happened. When I went to my last fire the creature was still be there, lurking on the fringes of my consciousness, exciting me, scaring me, and giving me purpose.

This Guy's Light

Other than the shower and bathroom there is probably no area in a firehouse that is more intimate than the kitchen. It is there that meals are prepared, stories are told, and personalities are forged.

Physically, it's a somewhat removed inner sanctum. The kitchen is usually located in the rear of the first floor and just getting access to it requires a bit of a journey. You enter a firehouse through large, open apparatus bay doors that dwarf you in size and usher you into a cavernous world of gleaming brass and enormous vehicles. Before you get any further you will meet a firefighter who is assigned to answer the phones, monitor alarms, and greet visitors. Like a bouncer in a 1920s speakeasy he will size you up and determine if you get to proceed any further. If you pass his inspection you will experience an abrupt transition as you pass through a garage-like section where fire trucks are parked to the area where food is prepared. A single door is often the only barrier between a pungent, gritty fire engine and a table full of delicacies.

Once inside, the atmosphere of smoke-scented firefighting equipment is immediately replaced by the essence of steak and potatoes. Large, industrial-type stoves compete for space with equally enormous tables where the appetites of ravenous firefighters are sated. Racks of pots, pans, and colanders large enough to feed an army hang from the ceiling. The tiled walls amplify even the slightest sounds and ensure that nobody misses out on any significant complaints or rumors.

In some kitchens there may also be a television set hanging on a wall. The TV is likely to be playing regardless of whether anyone is even there. I have often gone into an empty kitchen after returning from a fire at 3 or 4 in the morning and been greeted by an ancient black and white episode of *The Honeymooners* or assaulted by a hyped-up salesman pushing a radically new type of cleaning rag (available at half price if you immediately call his toll free phone number).

The kitchen becomes a focal point immediately after returning from a fire, like a setting for a town hall meeting. It is a place to sit and gradually come down from the high of a successful operation. The fire is analyzed from a tactical perspective, lessons are reinforced, and, as always, dark humor is bantered about. Which civilian was a real pain in the ass at this job? Who was the hottest-looking female television reporter at the scene? Which chief has absolutely no idea what he is doing?

Firehouse food is traditional, tasty, and plentiful. Meals tend to be served late, particularly on busy days. Usually a later meal makes for a better meal as your churning stomach is tempted by the result of hours of roasting, simmering, and sautéing. When the meal is finally ready to be dished out, firefighters ladle out servings of food while someone carefully evaluates portion sizes and, in a Solomon-like manner, announces, "This guy's light" to indicate which plate has been shortchanged. Not that you will ever see airline-sized meals in a firehouse. Plates are typically loaded with mountains of gravy-laden potatoes and chicken cutlets that match your shoe size. The challenge lies not in getting enough but in forcing yourself to eat less.

The influence of the 1950s cookbook has long been evident in the fire service. In a sort of gastronomical time warp, fats and butters are liberally

The kitchen is the focal point of a firehouse. These Bronx firefighters are relaxing and discussing life at the kitchen table (photograph by Rich Alexander).

applied, meats and cheeses avidly consumed, and triglycerides largely ignored. But in recent years this has been changing. Many firefighters are now more enlightened nutrition-wise and most exercise regularly. Salads, fish, and fruit have made inroads though they are sometimes derided by traditionalists who insist that they want no part of that "yuppie shit."

Regardless of the nature of the food two basic mores are paramount in firehouse kitchen culture. First, you can never admit that you really liked the meal. No matter how good the food tasted, scatological comments and references to the cook's ineptitude are always appreciated. Second, no matter what the price of the meal is determined to be, one must always complain that it costs too much.

The sociology of the firehouse kitchen is hidden to the casual or uninitiated observer. However, the pecking order and subtle traditions are ever-present. There are two general branches in the fire service. Engine companies position and operate hoses to extinguish the fire. Ladder companies perform the search and rescue functions. They are complementary fireground tasks but they often breed competing cultures. In some kitchens engine firefighters and ladder personnel will sit at separate tables. I have even worked in a place where the engine and ladder units actually ate in separate kitchens, each suspiciously eyeing the other as an untouch-

Some of the kitchen tables are handmade works of art that reflect the pride of the unit (photograph by Rich Alexander).

able caste. At some tables places have been unofficially reserved for senior members who have been sitting in the same chair for decades. Brand new firefighters will often sit next to each other, ready to quickly spring up from the table and fulfill their role of being the first to finish eating and the last to stop cleaning up.

The most unusual kitchen relationship I witnessed was in a Bronx firehouse. Clara was part of the first group of female firefighters hired by the FDNY in the early 1980s, a development that was met with a great deal of resistance by many of the men on the job. She had previously been a grade-school teacher, was bright and competent and, most important of all, easy to get along with. It didn't take long for her to be accepted and fit in. She was initially assigned to the same firehouse as Johnny, a guy who looked very much like the classic image of a firefighter. Johnny was six-foot-two, young, and powerfully built. And in one of those strange quirks that make life interesting he had also been one of Clara's students when he was in grade school. Johnny had grown and changed significantly over the years but the essence of the teacher/student relationship had not. One evening he was tasked with figuring out the cost of the meal and determining how much each person had to pay, a relatively simple but somewhat tedious arithmetic problem. As he furiously scribbled numbers on a piece of paper Clara peered over his shoulder, warning, "This is 4th grade math, you better get it right!" I don't know if he came up with the right price but it was the only time I remember Johnny looking nervous.

While there were some cultural changes necessitated as the FDNY eased its way into the 21st century, one aspect of the firehouse world stayed the same. It continued to be a great place to be in if you savored sharp and biting humor. The firehouse kitchen was not a place for the faint of heart. Raucous laughter and hearty jokes bounced off the tiled walls with the subtlety of a sledgehammer smashing a fly. The humor was profound and profane and wielded in an atmosphere of unabashed political incorrectness. No ethnic group, political bent, or fire department rank managed to escape the stinging barbs. The kitchen served as the ultimate democratic equalizer: everybody and everything was a legitimate target.

When I was a firefighter my very experienced but somewhat strait-laced captain was giving us a drill on how to perform an effective search for victims inside a burning apartment. There were about 12 of us sitting around the kitchen table and we were feeling somewhat beaten up from the previous night tour.

"Guys," he said, "it's very important that you search in an orderly manner. Always know where you are and know where the exit is in case you have to suddenly get out. It's a hard and dangerous job and you have to learn to control your emotions," at which point someone in the back blurted out, "I love you!" It kind of went over the captain's head and he continued to drone on with the drill. But the line had me in stiches and highlighted the wise-ass ethos that was ever-present in most firefighters.

Occasionally civilian trainers were also introduced to the world of firehouse humor. One such person was assigned to show us a video about diversity in the fire service. The well-intended but somewhat naïve thinking was that a certain level of government-mandated training would make firefighters more receptive to the cultural changes that were being introduced to the job. The video was exceptionally well-produced and started out with a young man talking about how his firefighting uncle was his inspiration for joining the fire service. This was followed by a very attractive female firefighter discussing her job experiences and her appearance immediately drew out the comment "That's his uncle!" from the back of the room. I could tell that the trainer totally missed the transgender barb and I kind of felt for him because he seemed quite sincere but somewhat oblivious to the atmosphere he was working in.

The humor may have been loud and stinging but beneath it all you sensed a connection between firefighters that you are not likely to see in other jobs. I experienced some of my funniest moments in FDNY kitchens, and some of my most Kafkaesque. A few years ago my firehouse was experiencing a rodent problem. One evening I was enjoying a meal in the kitchen with about dozen other guys and one of my favorite firefighters happened to be working. Tony was one of the senior people in the company, a much-respected firefighter, and an accomplished chef. Whenever he cooked the meal you knew the food was likely to be Italian and was certain to be excellent. Tony was also a classic outspoken New Yorker compete with the "fuhgeddaboudit" accent. Picture a Joe Pesci–type character in a blue uniform. Tony would have been a good fit for *Goodfellas* and a lot of other New York–themed movies.

After finishing my meal I noticed that there was a mouse on the floor a few feet away from me and I slammed my foot down attempting to scare it. But this must have been a pretty tough mouse because much to my surprise it stood its ground and didn't move at all. Suddenly, I saw a blur moving out of the corner of my eye followed by a huge crashing sound. Tony had thrown his entire plate of food at the creature. The area where the mouse had chosen to make his stand was covered in pasta, tomato sauce, and melted mozzarella cheese. For a few seconds there was nothing but a stunned silence, one of the few such moments I ever experienced in the kitchen. Tony then broke the stillness and calmly stated, "Hey, the mouse disrespected the chief." His reasoning and actions were shocking, but how could you not appreciate such dedicated loyalty? And, yes, he did eliminate the mouse. Firefighters are, if nothing else, very practical individuals.

The firehouse kitchen is more than a place to eat. It's a social experience, an exercise in bonding, a testing ground, and a special place where firefighters retreat to unwind from the tedium and rigors of their work. And, despite my background, when I was growing up it's a place I never envisioned myself being in.

The 15/16ths Jewel

I grew up on the waterfront of the East River. Waterfront may sound appealing but it definitely wasn't the Hamptons. Brooklyn was not far from Manhattan but the glittering New York City skyline was on an entirely different planet that sat, distant and unreachable, over on the other side of the river. The Greenpoint section of Brooklyn was a stable but aesthetically challenged place. Factories hid most of the waterfront from the community and the old row frame dwellings that lined the streets hadn't changed much since they were built at the turn of the 20th century except for an occasional layer of new asphalt siding. And that was always accomplished in drab hues of gray or tan. Holiday lights dangled from the streetlamps at Christmastime and kielbasa hung in the store widows all the time. There were very few trees and no flowers except for the ones sold in the florist shop and the only harbinger of an approaching spring was the slow melting of the dirty mountains of plowed snow.

Generations of families lived there. Some were as embedded in the community as the old trolley tracks and cobblestones that sometimes peeked out from beneath the tar-covered streets. I never ran with the rougher gangs of kids that roamed the neighborhood but I played ball with just about all of them in those streets. And that gave me an unspoken immunity to the intimidation and assaults they occasionally bestowed on unsuspecting interlopers. Marlon Brando's *On the Waterfront* character, Terry Malloy, would have fit right in in the neighborhood.

I lived about a block from the river and there was a small park nearby located right on the waterfront. When I was about three or four years old I got to spend a lot of time there with my mother. The park was very small and triangular in shape, really more of a playground than anything else. It had the usual assortment of swings and slides and a small brick maintenance building. The large sycamore trees provided a tiny green oasis inside the cluster of lumber yards and factories that surrounded it.

One day in the middle of our usual park routine my father suddenly appeared. His fire engine was in the area and they were apparently just mopping up after extinguishing a small fire near the park. Since he worked in the neighborhood his presence wasn't that unusual but what he held in his hand certainly was. It was a polished brass hose nozzle that glittered in the afternoon sun, shining and brilliant like some kind of exotic jewel. I had never seen such an object before and I stared at it, mesmerized by its physical beauty and the way that it so contrasted with everything else around it. I remember thinking, "Dad, where did you get such a thing and what is it?"

What my father held was a 15/16ths nozzle, the workhorse tool in the trade of extinguishing fires. The number refers to the diameter of the nozzle outlet and a version of it is still in use today, only today's tool has an entirely different look and feel. Modern fire nozzles are made of aluminum and synthetic materials. They are generally black or gray in color, weigh less, and are not as physically tiring to use. Like so much else in the fire service newer is better in terms of performance and safety. But along with the advantages comes a loss of ambiance. The modern nozzle is a sleek, efficient Chevy Impala while the old one is a classic Model A. As a firefighter I fully welcomed new technology making my job easier but I never gave up an appreciation for the classic look of brass.

Not long ago I passed through the old neighborhood. I had some time to kill and, in a moment of spontaneous curiosity, decided to drive by the park.

The author at three years of age welcoming his father home from work (Dunne family photograph).

Surprisingly, not much had changed in the half century since I had played there as a child. The sycamore trees were larger than I remembered and a modern version of the playground equipment sat in the exact same positions where the old swings and slides had been. A thick layer of black rubber padding had been installed, no doubt to protect a small child from getting bruised and a big city from getting sued. The old lumber yard was gone and there was still some open land right on the river. I wondered how long it would be before yet another high rise would sprout up to house the spillover of rent-challenged Manhattanites who continued to pour into the area and inflate the housing values.

What struck me more than anything was what I hadn't seen as a child. The view from the park provided an amazing, crystal-clear vista of the mid–Manhattan skyline lying just across the river. It looked like a postcard that some excited tourist from Nebraska would send home to his friends. How could I have absolutely no memories of this? I guess it comes down to perspective. As a three-year-old my focus was on my mother and my tenuous grip on the chains that held the swing seat, and on the curious yellow bark that peeled from the sycamores. I was oblivious to the world outside of my pocket park. An occasional glimpse of a passing airplane, steaming tugboat, or gleaming hose nozzle might interrupt my myopic point of view but skyline gazing was an adult passion and even adults eventually lost interest if they saw it too often.

I decided to stay for a while and enjoy the view. And as I sat there I thought about time and change and brass nozzles.

The Scuttle

I spent my first year on the job working in an engine company in the borough of Queens. Over that time I caught a number of good jobs, as fires are referred to in the FDNY, and grew more comfortable with both the nature of the work as well as the radically new culture I found myself in. In many ways the work was easier to adapt to than the culture. Most of the old-timers I worked with were very conservative, extremely boisterous, and really loved their beer. They were solid, blue collar guys that I mostly liked but had a hard time relating to. I was quiet, somewhat cerebral, and wasn't a big drinker. And even though my father had been a firefighter and I had been exposed to the job at an early age, the firehouse world was not an easy fit for me. Years of working and socializing with so-called "professionals" had made me kind of narrow minded in my own way if not outright cynical.

I was kind of amazed and alienated by some coworkers who were deeply parochial, staunchly religious, or extremely right wing in their politics. I never told anyone that I had graduated from college and understood that my previous education was totally irrelevant in my new work world. However, somehow the word got out that I had a degree and I was instantly advised by one old, irritable dinosaur to stick my diploma up my ass. He, however, was the exception. Despite our differences in style and personality I was easily accepted by most firefighters since I was a model probie. I fully understood my lowly position in the fire department pecking order so I did what I was told and I did it quickly and well. The truth was I liked the work and enjoyed learning about the job and I think my positive approach was appreciated.

After the first year I was longing for a change of scenery from the neighborhood I started in and wondered what it would be like to work in the hustling world of mid–Manhattan. I mentioned this to one of the senior guys that I really liked. He was on the tail end of his career and had worked all of it in the Bronx and Queens. The one regret he had was not having been assigned in Manhattan. With his encouragement my mind was set and I was ready for the big move.

I also wanted to work in a ladder company and learn "truck" work to round out my firefighting experience. The truck guys got to use a lot of neat tools and had a wide variety of fireground tasks. They were also the "shock troops" who entered a building to perform searches and rescue victims, often before the hose line was even in position. The initial "one year and out" mentality I had when I first started the job had been replaced by a desire to really challenge myself and develop into a solid FDNY firefighter.

So I wound up in a mid–Manhattan truck company and the change couldn't have been more extreme. Initially, it was kind of overwhelming and there was a lot to learn. There were five firefighters and an officer on each ladder company and your specific assignment varied according to the type of incident, the construction of the building, and the order in which your unit arrived at the scene of a fire. Aside from the firefighting tasks the entire work environment was also radically different. I had become accustomed to a quiet commercial and residential response area and now I was immersed in a maelstrom of high rises and noisy streets crowded with traffic and pedestrians. My firehouse in Queens was near a cemetery. My new one seemed like it was in the center of the universe. And I loved being there.

Over the first year in Manhattan my confidence grew and I looked forward to going to work every day to learn and experience something new. One autumn afternoon I wasn't feeling all that well while I was at home and getting ready to go to work. I had a really bad cold but didn't want to call in sick. Going on sick leave in the FDNY wasn't like calling in to an office job and telling them that you were ill and you'd be back at work the next morning. If, for any reason, you were put on medical leave in the fire department you had to be examined by a department doctor before you could be cleared to return to work. This meant a long trip down to the FDNY medical office which was located in an area of the city that was very inconvenient to get to. Most of our doctors were pretty good but if at all possible you generally wanted to avoid going there. Instead, you just tried to get through a tour and recoup on your own time at home. My ladder company was pretty busy and tended to do a lot of running around but I figured it was just a bad cold. I thought I'd pace my way through the night tour and, most likely, nothing big would happen. I didn't realize that I had set myself up to experience another case of Murphy's Law in action.

What was going to happen during that night tour was lying in wait on East 22nd Street. It was an enormous, six-story residential building that contained more than one hundred apartments. Like many old Manhattan buildings it had a history. Back in the 19th century it had actually been comprised of six separate factory occupancies and had undergone an extensive renovation in the 1970s that transformed it into one large apartment building. Most of the time when something like that happens it is good news for realtors and apartment-seekers and really bad news for firefighters. The exterior of the building was brick but the renovation process had transformed the wooden interior into a honeycomb of vertical and horizontal void spaces that were ideally placed to allow for the rapid spread of fire and smoke. The structural transformation had been designed for profit but the building had been built to burn, a sort of "perfect storm" just waiting to happen. It would turn out to be the site of the most difficult fire I had yet faced. But beyond that it would present a strong dose of the harsh realities of life and death and fundamental questions about courage and commitment. And, of course, I was oblivious to all of this as I drove to work.

The alarm came in around 5 in the morning, a time when bad things often seemed to occur in the firefighting world. When my unit arrived at the scene the fire had already spread throughout the building and into the roof area. My assignment was to cut holes in the roof to allow the smoke and heat to escape the upper portions of the building. The aerial ladder was the only safe way to get up there and so, laden with all my tools and equipment, I started the long climb. I had a heavy power saw slung over my shoulder, an axe and a stout metal "halligan" tool in my right hand, and my 30-pound Scott air pack on my back. Only my left hand was free and I used it to steady myself on the ladder which bounced gently beneath me as I climbed.

Needless to say, burdened with all of that weight I was exhausted by the time I finally reached the roof level which stood some 60 feet above the street. And once I got up there my work had just begun. Because of my illness I already felt like crap and I quietly cursed myself for not calling in sick as I should have. This was not shaping up as the relatively easy night tour I had hoped for. I threw my tools down on the roof and paused for a few seconds to catch my breath. There were already a dozen or more firefighters up there who were heavily engaged in trying to vent the smoke out of the building. I was surprised to see that there were also two building residents, a man and a woman, squatting together in a smoke-free section of the roof. They caught my eye because there was something very unusual in their appearance. I couldn't quite put my finger on it but, aside from the fact that their presence was completely incongruous with the whole roof scene, they looked like they were shell-shocked. At this point in my career I had seen people who had been injured and victims who had been killed. This was different. The couple were in an extreme state of psychological distress that showed in their physical demeanor. They must have made their way to the roof prior to the arrival of the fire department to escape the stinging smoke that had suddenly invaded their apartment. And I understood exactly how they felt. Imagine being abruptly transitioned from the peace and privacy of sleeping in your bed to the frightening public exposure of a smoke-filled roof and then being surrounded by the confusion and noise of a firefighting operation. It took just a few seconds to note all of this but once I caught my breath I put it aside and went to work.

To accomplish my ventilation task I had to use the power saw that I had so painfully lugged up the aerial ladder in my climb to the roof. It was gas fueled and had a circular steel blade that spun rapidly and could easily cut into the tar covered wooden roof surface. It kind of looked like a carpenter's skill saw on steroids but instead of producing the high-pitched whine you might hear on a construction site it sounded more like a Harley Davidson, and an especially loud one at that. The saw was a big, powerful machine designed to make quick, rough cuts in thick roof surfaces under difficult conditions. The roof saw was not to be messed with. It lacked the subtlety of the tools I had used when I did carpentry jobs and if it was not used properly it could do some damage to both the operator and to anyone standing nearby. With one hefty pull on the starting cord I turned it on and it immediately added to the ear-splitting noise level on the roof.

I didn't have all that much experience actually using the saw at that point in my career so I worked slowly, carefully monitored the depth and direction of my cuts, and tried to concentrate in spite of all the background noise. As I leaned over and directed the saw my entire focus was on watching the spinning blade as it tore into the roof surface. For several minutes I maintained the same view. It was just me and my saw blade ripping long cut lines that threw back wooden splinters, coated my boots with a spray of roof tar, and instantly released dark smoke from below. I forgot about my illness and the frightened couple I had just seen cowering nearby and even felt a surge of energy as my adrenaline kicked in. I was totally immersed in the task and my senses concentrated on the smoke that pushed from my cuts, the scent of the roof tar, and the noise of my saw.

I had finished the first round of cutting and was in the process of inspecting my work when my focus was suddenly and dramatically interrupted. Out of the corner of my eye I saw a firefighter's head pop up out of an open roof hatchway about 15 feet from where I was standing. The hatchway, or "scuttle" as it was called in the fire service, had been opened up to act like a chimney and help relieve conditions on the floor below. The firefighter was hovering right in the middle of the opening immersed in a cloud of thick black smoke. He abruptly ripped off the face piece of his air mask and yelled out, "There's a fireman dying down below!"

Everything changed in an instant and I was no longer centered on

A well-executed roof cut allows smoke, fire, and heat to escape from the building (photograph by the author).

my work or the fact that I didn't feel so well or even that I was standing on the roof of a burning building. With that remarkable human capacity to engage numerous different thoughts in a split second my mind was filled with a sudden blast of existential reality and deep-seated fear. A firefighter was actually dying. That meant that I could die, a fact I had accepted on an intellectual plane but never on a realistic, feeling level. I had perceived death as something that happens to fire victims, and that meant civilians, the people we rescue. Somehow, despite all the statistics on firefighter deaths, *we* were not supposed to die in a fire. We knew the harsh rules of the fireground and how to play the game and survive. The excitement of my first two years on the job had masked certain aspects of reality. Here was my first authentic confrontation with the prospect of dying in the performance of the job. And my mind was screaming, "What am I doing here?"

All of these thoughts were spinning through my head in the few seconds it took to walk over to the firefighter in the scuttle. His presence there added to the surreal aspect of it all. There was no way that a guy was supposed to just suddenly appear in the midst of a smoking scuttle opening. It had been drilled into us over and over in our training that you *never* went into a scuttle while a fire was being fought below. That was a prime route for fire, smoke, and heat to vent up and out of the building. To go down there was a certain path to getting seriously injured or killed.

The scuttle was about three feet wide and laid flush with the roof surface. The opening provided direct access to the floor below by means of a metal ladder that was permanently positioned in a vertical 90-degree angle. It was certainly not a prime means of egress and it would have been a chore to climb up or down the ladder even if dense smoke was not flowing past it. Yet here was this firefighter standing on that ladder with his head sticking above the roof and he was anxiously communicating the worst possible message. This had become much more than an opening in the roof. It was a pathway into a level of danger I had never experienced before, an encounter that would require a level of commitment I wasn't sure I had.

One of the senior men in my company was facing me as he stood on

These firefighters have just opened up the roof. Roof cuts, scuttle openings and skylights will allow the fire to vent but can also create a severe hazard to anyone who is positioned in the wrong location (photograph by Chris Creighton).

the opposite side of the scuttle. He was a really nice guy that I had grown to like and respect in the time we had worked together. A veteran of many years on the job, he was knowledgeable, had an extensive fire background, and was generally a pleasure to hang out with. However, I could readily tell from his facial expression that he was as alarmed by the situation as I was. I looked at him and he looked back at me, and in that brief instant when you just know what a person is thinking, I knew that he had absolutely no intention of going down that scuttle ladder to help out below. His obvious decision just added to my fear. With all of his experience, if he wasn't going to try to assist in rescuing the firefighter, I knew that this must be a really bad situation.

I don't remember giving it any thought. If I had stopped and just rationalized it I probably would have done nothing. But for reasons I can't fully explain I next found myself inside the scuttle opening groping for the ladder with my extended leg. And though I was breathing through the face piece of my air pack I can't even remember pausing to put it on. But there I was, slowing climbing down the scuttle ladder in zero visibility surrounded by thick smoke. I was stretching the envelope and I knew it. I wasn't even sure precisely what I was going to do, just that *something* had to be done even if I had no real plan. And the fact that I had no plan reflected my inexperience. This was virgin territory for me. I tried to beat down that inner voice that was yelling, "What the hell are you doing?" by forcing myself to think, "Just keep moving, just keep moving."

And I did keep moving. Once I had climbed down the scuttle ladder and reached the floor below it was very quiet and almost peaceful, a stark contrast to the noise and confusion of the roof area. All I could hear was my own breathing which was amplified by the mechanical diaphragm of my air mask. It was kind of like walking on the bottom of the ocean, only instead of water I was surrounded by smoke. I had moved about 10 feet away from the scuttle ladder when it suddenly dawned on me that I was advancing in zero visibility and it would be very easy to entirely lose my sense of direction. If I couldn't find my way back to the scuttle area I could easily become helplessly trapped myself. Instead of assisting in a rescue I had put myself in a hazardous position that might make me yet another firefighter who desperately needed help. While my intention was good my inexperience once again showed. In my quick and unplanned effort at helping I had neglected to bring a search rope which I could have tied to the bottom of the scuttle ladder and used to guide me to a safe means of egress.

I immediately turned around and cautiously groped my way back to the scuttle area and was instantly relieved once I felt the secure feeling of holding the metal ladder in my gloved hand. With a mental image of where I was and where I had to go I turned around again and proceeded to reenter the smoke-filled top-floor hallway, only this time I remembered to keep my left hand on the wall next to me. Now I had at least established a path back to safety. That wall would be my guide if I had to suddenly escape back up to the roof.

Feeling reassured I moved forward and groped through the smoke with my right hand. I tried to fight down my anxiety and control my breathing since I had, at best, about 15 minutes of air in my mask to get in, make the search, and get out. Each of my breaths was amplified in the confines of my mask face piece and seemed to be repeating, "You're running out of time, you're running out of time." And it was hard to judge time since I was having that peculiar sensation you get of time slowing down when you are under stress. I was operating entirely on my own and I had never felt more alone in my entire life.

I must have been moving for just a few minutes when I saw him. There, right in front of me, was a firefighter. He had his back to me and was leaning over with his face toward the floor looking very much like he was sick or about to pass out. I immediately grabbed him from the rear in a bear hug with as much strength as I could muster. He was fairly big and with the air tank on his back it was difficult to get a really good grip on him. I had no idea how far I could drag him or how I could possibly get him up the scuttle ladder. But I knew exactly where that scuttle was and since I had just gone through it myself I figured it would be the most direct escape route. So I squeezed him with everything I had and started tugging backwards.

Wearing a mask face piece does more than force you to hear your own breathing. It also makes it very hard to communicate with the people around you. Even up close the best you can hope for is an extremely muffled voice no matter how loud you are speaking. The firefighter I had grabbed had his face piece on and as soon as I started pulling on him I heard a barely audible "It's not me! It's not me!" I immediately realized that in the darkness of the smoke I had not located a "victim" but one of the rescuers. This guy had made an aggressive search through the hallway, located the downed firefighter, and was assisting him when I stumbled upon him. After a split second of embarrassment I felt a real sense of relief. I wasn't by myself. There were other firefighters already here, not doubt with more experience than I had, and that meant that the incapacitated firefighter was going to be removed to a safe position where he could receive medical treatment.

Someone on the roof passed a rope down through the scuttle opening and it was used to haul up the downed firefighter. When I eventually climbed back up to the roof myself I was physically exhausted and emotionally relieved. The man had been recovered and I was safe. I was back in the daylight and breathing clean air. That firefighter survived. And in a kind of poetic irony 25 years later when I was a deputy chief assigned to the Bronx his son was one of the men working for me.

When it was all over I still liked the senior guy from my company who had chosen not to act and continued to think of him as a decent man. In fact, I kind of understood his perspective. He was older than I was and nearing the end of his career. He also had a child to care for. I was single and responsible for no one but myself. I wonder how I would have reacted to the same situation later on in my life when I had children of my own. But I did lose some of the naïve view I had held for the pecking order of the firehouse. Time on the job meant a lot but it did not necessarily guarantee that you could rely on someone in a tight situation. And as I reevaluated the whole concept of seniority I realized that my own capability had been raised a notch.

That idea was reinforced when I went back to work on my next tour. As soon as I got into the firehouse someone mentioned that I did a good job with the rescue and another guy even felt that I should have gotten a medal for my efforts. I merely responded that it had been a really difficult fire and didn't make a big deal of it. Of course, I didn't tell them that I had attempted to "rescue" someone who wasn't even a victim. Nonetheless, I knew I had done my best despite my fear and it felt good to hear their comments. And the incident was a significant point in my growing confidence as well as my position in the company.

When I look back on this experience I think less about what I did and more about why I went down that scuttle without hesitating. I am not an especially courageous man although I've worked with a few who truly were. It certainly wasn't peer pressure because no one else on that roof made a move. Was I motivated by subconscious remnants of the rigid rule-following Roman Catholic background that I thought I had totally rejected? Perhaps I was acting in accord with my perceived notion of how a "firefighter" should act. Or it may be as simple as I feared the danger less than the embarrassment of failing to do what I knew in my soul to be the only acceptable course of action.

Which leads to the question of defining what courage really is. Is it a precise and rigid concept? Maybe it's just another word for trying to do the right thing even when you are scared shitless.

The Wrapper

One of the fascinating things about being a firefighter in the FDNY was the sense of history that was ever-present in both the city and the fire department. There were layers of past life lying just beneath the surface that were occasionally revealed by modern construction projects. Old ships, ancient burial grounds, and the foundations of original Dutch dwellings sometimes popped up when an excavation was begun for a new high-rise building. The department itself was deep-rooted, dating back to 1865. Some of the fire houses were more than one hundred years old and with just a little imagination you could catch a glimpse of what life was like in the 19th century.

Very often you could view that historical perspective by leafing through the company journals. If you walked into any fire house today, or did so back in the 19th century, the first person you would encounter would be the "house watchman." That would be a firefighter sitting at a desk who is responsible for guarding the property, receiving alarms, and recording the day's events in a large, bound company journal. The journal has not changed much in appearance in more than a century. It is a heavy book with hard covers and looks much like an account ledger that Ebenezer Scrooge would scribble in with a quill pen. The journal is an official listing of all the alarms the company responds to, an accounting of the personnel that are on duty, and a record of mundane items such as heating oil deliveries (or, in the older journals, the status and feeding times of the assigned horses).

I occasionally got to work in some of the really old Manhattan fire-houses and though they were 20th-century occupancies they managed to retain a 19th-century soul. The brass poles, high ceilings, and ancient woodwork all looked original. And if you looked closely you could still make out where the horse stalls and coal bins had been located. Whenever I worked in one of the older places I was always on the look-out for any original company journals that might be squirreled away in some ancient cabinet or stacked up in a musty corner of a seldom explored loft area. Sometimes I would uncover a moldy bunch of them in the basement or discover a dusty collection sitting on an attic shelf where they may have been lying undisturbed for decades. When I approached these journals the history behind them would actually bombard my senses. If a time warp had a scent it would smell just the way these books did.

The first thing that hit me when I leafed through the pages of the old journals was the difference in penmanship. Most of the entries in modern books are filled with pages of indecipherable ballpoint pen scratches. In contrast, the yellowing pages of 19th-century journals revealed endless lines

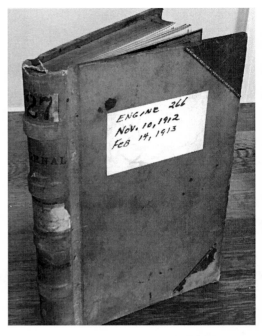

A company journal from 1912. The book hasn't changed much in appearance in more than a century (photograph by the author).

of perfect, artistic penmanship that were precisely crafted with painstaking flourishes. They looked more like they were written by a calligrapher than by a firefighter. I don't know if they had a lot of time on their hands in the 19th century or if our fingers just can't keep up with today's multimedia-induced brain distractions.

One day while working in a mid–Manhattan firehouse I hit pay dirt on one of my archeological quests. I came across a journal from 1873 which was by far the oldest I had yet uncovered. As I carefully leafed through the book I reached a section that had a shiny piece of silver foil tucked between two pages. The foil looked brand new and I assumed that it was a modern candy wrapper or perhaps a piece of aluminum foil that had been casually disposed of at some point when the contents of the firehouse were rearranged for spring cleaning. However, when I looked closely I saw that the piece of foil was actually a 19th-century tobacco wrapper.

You can talk all you want about books, lectures, or plays about George Washington, Alexander Hamilton, or the Civil War. To me there is no more interesting way of sensing history than a tactile experience of everyday, mundane items that were part of the lives of ordinary people in the past. Here I was handling something that another firefighter routinely used 112 years ago while he was doing the same job in the exact same place I was now. The page that had hidden the wrapper all those years was dated August 11, 1873. I glanced at a written entry on that page which noted that fireman David McBride had assumed the role of house watchman at 6 a.m. Who was he and what was he like? Had he been suddenly distracted by something and was he very tired at that early hour? In my mind I pictured him filling his pipe with tobacco, closing the journal with the wrapper inside, and then walking away to attend to the horses. Only to have me uncover the same wrapper in the next century.

I got increasingly curious the more I thought about fireman David McBride and his distant world. When he was a firefighter the FDNY had only been in existence for eight years. There is a good chance that he was a Civil War veteran. There was no Brooklyn Bridge and Ulysses S. Grant was the president of what was then the United States. Colorado, Montana, Arizona, and a host of other western territories were years away from statehood. And when David wrote his routine entries in the journal George Armstrong Custer was gallivanting about out west in a fringe buckskin jacket oblivious to his fate on the Little Big Horn which wouldn't occur for another three years.

We have a tendency to view 19th-century people as quaint, mustachioed, black-and-white entities devoid of the

Firefighter David McBride made his journal entry on August 11, 1873, in his impeccable 19th-century handwriting (photograph by the author).

excitement, boredom, and pleasures that we now experience. Yet here was a guy who was performing the same house watch duties as me. And like me he may have been a bit bored with the task so he smoked to pass the time and to stay awake just as I would sip a cup of 20th-century coffee when I was the house watchman. I almost felt like I knew the guy. As if the tobacco wrapper somehow bridged a century and I could ask him how his night tour had gone and what he thought of the big news about the Boss Tweed scandal.

But I pictured David McBride's firehouse as being a place with different values than I was accustomed to and an ambiance that would be alien to me. When he responded to an alarm, lumbering horses with names like Zachariah, Sweet Girl, Blackie, and Doc would automatically leave their stalls, line up to be harnessed, and pull a rig with large spoked wheels through a massive, hand-operated wooden door. And while his rig performed the same function it was quite primitive when compared to my modern, diesel-spewing apparatus.

While I was in the middle of contemplating these 19th-century images an alarm came in and I had to immediately leave for a 20th-century response. I carefully folded up the foil wrapper and slid down the pole to the apparatus floor. It was safely tucked away in my pocket as we sped through the congested Manhattan streets. There was something poetic about the fact that the tobacco wrapper was going on its first response in more than a century.

Of course, the ladder truck I responded on had a very different look and sound than the one David McBride rode in 1873. The noise alone would have spooked his horses, given the ear-splitting decibel level of a modern air horn. But despite the differences our tasks were essentially the same, to swiftly deliver that ladder rig to a place where it could be used to assist someone in distress. The 100-foot aerial ladder sitting on top of my fire truck was a hydraulic masterpiece capable of being set up and smoothly deployed in just minutes. His ladder would have been raised by a hand crank and it would have taken much longer to position it to make a rescue. However, I think the actual experience of climbing the ladder would have been pretty much the same.

When I started on the job the very first thing I ever did in probie school was climb an aerial ladder to the top of a five-story building. I took to it right away. In fact I always felt relatively comfortable with heights which I guess is a good thing to be if you want to be a firefighter. As with every other fireground evolution I learned that there was a right way and a wrong way to climb the ladder. My previous climbing experience had been limited to using a step ladder to paint a ceiling and I assumed that a long aerial ladder on a fire truck would just be a natural progression of that. However, we were trained to keep our hands on the metal rails that ran along the side of the aerial rather than actually griping the rungs of the ladder and this took some getting used to. Naturally, the steeper the angle of the aerial the more difficult it became to maintain this technique. In addition, a really good truck chauffeur would place the tip of the ladder just a couple of inches above a windowsill rather than directly on it. That allowed your body weight to force the tip of the ladder down on the sill and secured it once you got to the top. Of course, that also meant that the ladder would bounce slightly when you got up to the highest position, a movement that added to the anxiety of the whole experience. The sight of someone maintaining a tight grip on the rungs was a sure sign of a nervous and inexperienced ladder climbing novitiate. The key to establishing a comfort level was to just climb, develop a feel for it, and not obsess too much about what exactly it was you were doing. You absolutely could not think about the fact that the slender tendons in your wrist were the only things that were keeping you from falling.

It wasn't long before I mastered the ability to scurry up an aerial ladder with rhythm and confidence and I had images of using my newly-developed skill to rescue someone. However, I would eventually learn that a complete mastery of the art of lifesaving would also require an ability to determine when it was *not* possible to use a 100-foot ladder and that there were times when making a rescue would rely less on tools and more on the use of empathy and psychology.

Each of the five firefighters in a ladder company was assigned a specific responsibility for every tour. The forcible entry team consisted of

Looking down from the top of an aerial ladder. The steeper the angle the more difficult the climb (photograph by Louis Sclafani).

two firefighters who worked under the immediate supervision of the company officer. They would enter the building with the officer to determine the location of the fire and initiate the search for victims. The roof man was responsible for getting to the top of the building where he would create openings in the roof that provided vertical paths for the smoke to vent out of the building. The outside vent man or "OV" assisted the unit chauffeur in positioning the ladder truck and visually checked for any residents who were trapped at windows or on fire escapes. If there were people in distress it was the OV who climbed up the ladder and assisted them down to the street, hopefully without meeting with too much physical resistance from the people they were rescuing.

As I gained more experience I started getting assigned to the roof and OV positions. I enjoyed those roles because they called for an ability to work independently and make decisions without the immediate supervision of an officer. I had a radio that allowed me to communicate with other firefighters at the scene but I basically moved on my own, sized up problems, and figured out solutions to the obstacles that I inevitably ran into.

I was the OV one weekday afternoon when an alarm came in for a fire in an apartment building. Before we even left the firehouse I could tell from the tone of the dispatcher's voice that it was going to be a good job. He informed us that he was receiving numerous phone calls from the address, a clear sign that we were going to work. Our unit normally did a lot of running in mid–Manhattan but many of those responses were for minor incidents or false alarms. After responding on 15 to 20 runs riding on the truck became somewhat routine and guys would engage in conversation or exchange comments about the women we passed by in the street. The tone was entirely different when you knew you were going to a fire. As my adrenalin was pumping I performed a last-minute check of my air mask, radio, and tools and anxiously awaited the radio report from the first unit that would arrive at the fire. I tried to imagine a picture of the scene we were going to and mentally reviewed what I might encounter and what fireground tactics would be called for. Once the first arriving unit transmitted a "10–75" radio signal, signifying a working fire, it was like the opening kickoff of a football game and you knew it was really on. I was always most nervous before I got to the scene of an incident. Once I was there and could actually view the situation, size up the fire, and start to work, I generally felt a strange but reassuring sense of calm and control, kind of like what a boxer might feel when he finally takes his first hit in the ring.

When we arrived, dense, dark smoke was pushing from an upper floor in the front of the building. I immediately hustled off the rig to help the chauffeur position the truck and scanned the windows for trapped residents. There was a report of a woman in distress at a window adjacent to the room that was burning. I couldn't see her from the street but what I did immediately see was unnerving. The fire was so high up that any chance of approaching it from the outside would require positioning the aerial ladder at an extremely steep angle. This would be no graceful, rhythmic climb but a scary, cling-to-the-rungs ascent with the hope that, if the woman was up there, she wouldn't resist my efforts to help her and cause both of us to fall to our deaths.

The truck chauffeur was a very experienced guy who had been in the company for a long time and had seen a lot. He had an intimate knowledge of the buildings in our response area and he knew the capabilities of his truck. When I turned to him and asked if he thought he could reach the window with the aerial he just calmly replied no, it was beyond the reach of the 100-foot ladder. Naturally I felt an instant sense of relief at being spared what would have been an exceptionally dangerous climb and I immediately entered the building to find another way of checking for this woman.

I managed to get into an apartment adjacent to where she was supposed to be located and when I looked out the window, sure enough, there she was. I was probably no more than 10 feet from her and she was clearly frightened. The fire was ripping in the apartment right door next to her, there was a haze of smoke in her unit, and she was trying to escape the smoke by keeping her head outside a window that was 11 stories above the street. Given the construction of this particular building I knew that there was only a minimal chance that the fire would extend to her apartment. The engine was in the process of operating the hose line and within minutes the fire was going to be knocked down and the dark, threatening smoke would be replaced by a steamy white cloud that would be quickly vented away from the building. She was in no immediate danger and if she could just hold on for a few minutes she was going to be fine and would be able to enter the public hallway and make her way down to the street.

Of course I knew all this because I had seen it many times before and understood what would happen. She had no way of knowing. This was no doubt the first fire she had ever been in, she was breathing in some smoke and was, understandably, feeling scared and desperate. I felt really bad for her and as I leaned out of my own window I made eye contact with her and tried to ease her fear and provide some much-needed reassurance. Using my best "sensitive therapist" voice I told her my name and explained exactly what was happening in the burning room next door. I explained that the fire was being contained and extinguished as we spoke and that she was in no immediate danger and very soon she would be able to safely leave her apartment. I also assured her that I was absolutely not going to leave her until the whole thing was over.

While I continued my conversation with her I maintained radio contact with the chief who was supervising from the street as well as the units operating inside the fire apartment so that they were aware of the woman's exact location. It was kind of a strange position to be in. I was used to getting beaten up whenever I worked at a fire and here I was in a safe, comfortable, smoke free position totally divorced from the physical action. Yet, at the same time, I knew that I was playing an important role for this lady.

As expected, after a few intense moments I could hear on my radio that the fire had been knocked down and the woman safely removed from her precarious position at the window. She was OK but had to be taken down to the street to be evaluated by EMS. One of the members of my unit knew that I had established a sort of relationship with her and wanted me to be the one to guide her down. It was a small thing but I felt kind of honored that I was the one requested to assist her. Someone draped a blanket over her head to protect her from the dripping water and remaining haze and I gently took her arm and guided her to the elevator. I left her under the care of the EMTs in the street and advised the chief that she was out of the building.

Later on my company officer told me that the chief said I did a good job. And it did feel good to get the positive feedback. But the truth is, as far as "rescues" go, this one was a walk in the park. I had been not been placed in danger. I had taken no smoke and had not been directly exposed to the fire. I had merely reassured a person at a time when she really needed some reassurance. That being said, I felt like I had accomplished something good. The whole affair had probably taken no more than 20 minutes but for the lady involved it must have felt like an eternity. It would be recorded as just another incident in the 150-year history of the FDNY and I suspect that old David McBride would have had many similar tales to tell.

I keep David's tobacco wrapper tucked away in a protective plastic cover. I'm hoping that it will be found in one hundred years by someone who, like me, has a nerd-like interest in historical artifacts. But right now it sits on my desk as I am writing this. Only two men have handled it in the last 144 years and I guess that puts David and me in a pretty exclusive club. However, he and I share more than the possession of a piece of foil. We both had an opportunity to be a part of a great tradition. Along with the fun, excitement, and financial benefits of the job we both knew that we were doing something that could make a difference. Every tool, every procedure, and, yes, every aerial ladder we had was used for the sole purpose of helping someone in distress. And whether you did in 1873 or 1985 there were times when being a firefighter made you feel really good.

The Guys (and Gals)

People like firefighters. Or at least they like their concept of a fire-fighter, though sometimes that concept is shaped and influenced by childhood stories and *Sesame Street* images. The truth is that most people don't give much thought to the fire department or really know a lot about the people in it. Nonetheless, we are generally viewed as the good guys who are always there to help as opposed to the cops who are there to arrest you.

I actually like police officers. When I became a chief and managed large emergency operations they were always there to help with traffic control and site security. Cops and firefighters were the same kinds of guys and generally had very similar backgrounds and attitudes. They often took the same New York City civil service exams and wound up being employed by the first agency that offered them a job. A lot of the people I worked with started out as New York City cops and eventually transferred to the FDNY. In fact, I often pictured a police officer as firefighter who happened to be carrying a gun.

Most of the real confrontations between the police and fire departments occurred at the higher levels of our respective bureaucracies when the NYPD and the FDNY competed for job responsibilities and budget allocations. At the local level there were the occasional flare-ups between the few hotheads who were to be found in both of our organizations. On one occasion a firefighter was arrested when police and fire units both responded to an auto accident and clashed over which agency was responsible for managing the incident.

But on a day-to-day, street-level basis, we got along well with each other. Every cop walking a beat knew that he was always welcome to enter the inner sanctum of any firehouse to have a cup of coffee, catch up on his paperwork, or just chew the fat and discuss how we were all getting fucked by the city. (A city must be a really promiscuous entity. I've visited fire stations throughout the United States, Canada, and England, and, though

41

the accents may change, a common theme of conversation is how they are getting screwed by their respective municipalities.)

However, most people have not experienced the inner workings of the fire world and understandably harbor a pretty innocent view of that realm. My wife worked for a major magazine for a number of years and once in a while I had a chance to attend its corporate parties. It was interesting to see how much that universe contrasted with my work world. Sometimes when I was asked what I did I would say I was a firefighter and get back, "That's very interesting, but what do you do for a living?" and I would start wondering what kind of hors d'oeuvres were around. Or they might ask if I slid down a pole and had a Dalmatian. That generally indicated that they were either honestly naïve or just biding their time until they could find someone more interesting or more connected to converse with and I knew that it was definitely time to locate the snack table.

The FDNY had well over 10,000 employees and it would probably be inaccurate to make any general statement on the nature or style of the people who worked for it. There was just so much variety in the many different personalities. However, it would be fair to say that, overall, firefighters tended to be very conservative individuals. Their upbringing and backgrounds were certainly a key in forming their values. But I also have a theory about people who work in jobs that place them in an intimate relationship with the forces of nature. Farmers, fishermen, and firefighters are all affected by powerful natural elements that are often beyond their control. Their success or failure at work, indeed, their very survival, can be determined by the potentially devastating effects of wind, water, and fire. In that kind of work environment it kind of makes sense that they would staunchly adhere to the procedures, techniques, and attitudes that always kept them alive and well in the past. Survival does not tend to encourage a liberal mindset.

In all honesty there were times when the rigid outlook of some of my coworkers got kind of annoying. I was once criticized for reading the *New York Times* rather than the much more conservative *Daily News* or *New York Post*. (Though I must admit that the predictably liberal *Times* editorials seemed to portray a consistent intolerance of opposing ideas. But it did have a great sports section). And one firefighter questioned my choice to purchase a Japanese car rather than an American brand. I didn't bother to point out to him that World War II was long over and that my particular Honda had actually been manufactured at a plant in Ohio which provided employment and benefits for a fellow union tradesman.

For most of my time on the job the department was predominantly Irish and Italian though aggressive efforts at hiring and promoting black, Hispanic, and female candidates eventually arose as a result of contentious legal battles. The majority of my coworkers were nonminority and many, like myself, had a family history with the FDNY. But I always felt that it was unfair to label it as a racist institution. It is true that, as in any group of people, there were some individuals who bore certain prejudices. And in many of the poor, rundown neighborhoods the closed apparatus bay doors acted as both a physical and cultural shield from the people who lived there. Yes, there were rare occasions when I heard the "n" word in the firehouse kitchen. But I also worked with an excellent black fire-fighter who consistently railed about the "annoying Jews" whenever we responded to a certain section of the Bronx.

However, the ultimate judgment of any firefighter was based on his attitude and efforts both in the firehouse and on the fireground. Once you were on the job your ethnic background didn't mean anything if you couldn't contribute to the teamwork that was so necessary to get the work accomplished. Individuals who could fit in became a part of the "house" regardless of their race. And those who were assholes were castigated and rejected through the harsh peer pressure of the firehouse whether they were Irish, Hispanic, or African American.

The firefighters I worked with generally had a tremendous sense of humor to go along with their conservative leanings. But, again, it would be a mistake to paint too narrow a picture of them. Most were great to be around, a few were miseries. The vast majority were solid, salt of the earth people and a select few were horrible individuals. Following is a partial list of what some of them had been or would eventually become: actor, law-yer, writer, accountant, priest, teacher, farmer, convicted child molester, chef, artist, male erotic dancer, architect, murderer, lecturer, drug dealer, jet fighter pilot. Unfortunately, I also worked with two who committed suicide and one who suddenly and mysteriously disappeared (rumor had it that it was mob related). Certainly a group far more diverse than the pole-sliding, dog-petting image some might expect.

A few of the people I met on the job seem to have found a permanent place in my memory and deserve a mention (I've changed their names to protect the not so innocent).

Roy was a special guy. On my very first day in a firehouse he was the only one among a group of salty veterans who actually took the time to introduce himself and teach me what to do. I came in as a new "probie" and total outsider with absolutely no idea of the normal routines. He ap-proached me rather than my having to seek him out. I clearly remember him saying, "These guys aren't going to show you anything" as he pro-ceeded to help lay out my gear and get me ready for my very first response on the engine. He had been around for a long time and still had a passion for the job. Not too many years later he died of a heart attack while fighting a fire in Brooklyn. As I proceeded through many years and several ranks in the FDNY I too enjoyed taking a moment to show the ropes to the new guy. I know Roy would have been pleased.

Chuck had the quickest and sharpest wit of anyone I ever met, in or out of the fire service. There was no way I could ever respond to or even keep up with the zing and pace of his humor and I much preferred to sit back and enjoy it from a distance. But it seemed like his humor was also his shield. I don't think anybody ever really got to know Chuck, including his girlfriend, and the nonstop shtick carefully guarded much of what must have been going on inside him. He was an excellent firefighter and highly intelligent. Chuck was also an alcoholic.

The FDNY that exists today is radically different from the one I joined years ago. It is now a job that has certainly been "cleaned up." Long ago beer flowed pretty freely in certain firehouses. During a period of intense fire activity all of the men worked exceptionally hard and a few of them drank. As one old-timer who broke me in put it, "In some places beer put out more fire than water," no doubt an unfair generalization but an interesting description of an issue that once existed.

That time had long past but apparently nobody bothered to tell Chuck. There were days he would start popping cold ones in the morning, and over the course of a 24-hour tour, he would progressively work his way through a couple of six-packs. Chuck was a big man and had an enormous capacity for alcohol. I never recall seeing him visibly affected by his brew and he was always reliable at a fire.

I liked Chuck and sensed that there was an essential goodness buried deep inside his muddled core. One day just he and I were together in the locker room and we had an interesting conversation. He looked at me with an honest but confused look on his face and said, "I don't get you, an Irishman who doesn't drink." I was somewhat taken aback and immediately sensed that this was the real, unadorned Chuck talking. I didn't know quite how to respond. First of all, even though I had an Irish last name, I was two generations removed from our first family immigrants and didn't identity at all with that culture. I was about as Irish as Jackie Chan. And I did in fact drink. A glass of white wine with fish, red with spaghetti and meatballs, and a couple of cold beers with pizza, but only when I was not working. Still, I understood his confusion. He and I worked well together in the same firehouse but we resided in different worlds.

Chuck has since retired from the job. I've heard that he is happy and has sworn off the booze completely. Way to go, Chuck.

Ike was probably my favorite person of all the people I met in the FDNY. He was bright and warm, a very good firefighter, and a gifted basketball player. He was a joy to know and hang out with and you knew it was going to be a good tour whenever he was working. The abilities he displayed on the basketball court and on the fireground were only exceeded by his gentle humility. Unlike a lot of talented people he was not at all elitist and was readily approachable by anyone who wanted to discuss firefighting, sports, or life.

There is one particular image of Ike that I still retain very clearly. We had a fire on the East side of mid–Manhattan one afternoon and he had worked for an extensive time inside the building. When I saw him in the street he looked like he had taken a real beating on the job. His turnout coat was covered with dirt from the hard physical work he had performed and he looked absolutely exhausted. Yet, fatigued as he was, he still managed to greet me with a smile despite the discomfort he must have felt from the dark snoot that was flowing down from his nose. I remember being so impressed by the dignity he showed with that one small gesture. That was Ike, just doing his job in a quiet, dedicated manner.

Ike could also be wickedly funny. But he had subtle wit that contrasted sharply with the usual raucous, knee-slapping firehouse humor. He was once interviewed by a group of civilians who were doing a survey on why people chose the type of work they did. When asked why he became a firefighter Mike responded with a straight face, "I like to sleep with men." I have this image of a bunch of confused researchers staring at each other unsure of what to make of his response and wondering just exactly what went on in the firehouse bunk room. But, again, that was Ike, always willing to make life a bit more absurd and humorous. When I met his family I could see how close he was to his wife and children and how much they also appreciated his style.

Ike was killed on 9/11. I still have a hard time comprehending 2,606 deaths in the World Trade Center. And it is even harder to get a mental handle on how he can just be gone.

Joe was a "square rooter." That's a derogatory term used in the firehouse to describe someone who always has an angle and is constantly looking out for themselves. Kind of like the guy who has you checking for your wristwatch after you shake hands with him. He was also not that bright. But he didn't suffer from the kind of dullness that might confuse the playwright Anton Chekhov with the guy who was the navigator of the starship *Enterprise* in the original *Star Trek* television show. No, his ignorance was the worst kind. For he had absolutely no idea how dense he really was. He wore his stupidity on his sleeve or, more accurately, in his mouth, as he constantly spewed out an endless barrage of insults and opinions that were based on anything but fact.

But I was less concerned with Joe's mental prowess than I was to his approach to the job. He was one of the few people I worked with who really didn't seem to care at all about the fire department. When an emergency response came in I would often see him sitting impassively on the engine without even bothering to put on his turnout gear as though he was just taking a ride in a taxi. And with his "What's in it for me?" attitude I made a point of never relying on him at a good job.

I eventually lost all contact with Joe but many years later I received a phone call from him when I was a deputy chief. As soon as I heard his voice my square rooter antenna lit right up and I immediately wondered what he was up to because I was sure he hadn't called to wish me a happy birthday. It turned out that he was seeking some kind of payout from the World Trade Center Victims Compensation Fund and he needed documentation proving that he had been at the site. He spoke of all the times he had worked for me down there and wanted me to write a letter indicating that he had performed a certain number of hours of service. Now I couldn't say for a fact whether he actually did work in the Trade Center rubble but I did know with absolute certainty that I had never seen him in the months I was there. Naturally I refused his request. Once a square rooter, always a square rooter.

Stan was an interesting guy. When you first saw him you would think he was anything but a firefighter. Somewhat on the short side and rather chubby, he looked like he would be more at home at an all-you-can-eat buffet for some bank clerk's retirement party rather than on the fireground. I worked with him on many occasions as I went through several different ranks and locations throughout the city. Stan was an acquired taste, kind of like a quirky television sitcom that you'd rather not watch but just can't get yourself to turn off. Initially I completely ignored him. Then I found myself somewhat alienated by his antics. As I got to know him better I started to enjoy both him and his humor. Eventually I discovered that he was one of those hidden gems who had far more depth and ability than you might expect.

Stan was somehow able to perform very effectively as an excellent fire officer and a court jester at the same time. He broke many of the classic rules of supervision yet still earned a healthy respect from his firefighters. They would often call him by his first name, a definite "no-no" in any quasi-military organization. I think he loved the attention he got from his slapstick performances which broke up the kitchen routine like a comic relief act in a Shakespearean play. Rather than hiding his gargantuan appetite he would often make a public announcement about the massive amount of potatoes or meat he was about to add to his plate just to entertain the troops who, whether they admitted it or not, really loved him.

He was also one of the most reliable fire officers I knew and he provided a calm and steady influence you could count on at even the most difficult fires. Stan was proof that it was not always the guy with the biggest biceps who made the best firefighter but the one with the biggest heart.

In the early 1980s a new development rocked the FDNY to its very core. It had nothing to do with radical changes to safety equipment or alterations to the firefighting procedures that had served us for so long. No, it was far more basic (and, to some, more upsetting) than that. After a long and contentious legal battle women were hired as firefighters for the first time in the 117-history of the department. The old boys' club had not ended but it was about to change. It would be hard to overstate the repercussions that followed. No unpopular mayor, prolonged contract negotiation, or disliked fire commissioner ever caused more upset and debate in the firehouse kitchen.

That debate also spilled beyond the world of the firehouse. When I would meet civilians the first question they often asked me was "Do you think that women can do the job?" I could usually tell what answer they were looking for before I even opened my mouth to respond. At one social gathering I was approached by a woman who knew that I was a firefighter and, sure enough, out popped the big question. I recall that she was wearing Birkenstocks, carrying a Corporation for Public Broadcasting tote bag, and had the intense look of someone who had passionately digested every line that Gloria Steinem had ever written. She also mentioned how very impressed she was by a magazine article that had mentioned how hard one of the women trained for her fire department physical (as had I, though nobody wrote about it). It was very obvious which political direction she was coming from and what kind of answer she was seeking.

A few days later I got the same inquiry from an out-of-town volunteer firefighter who lived the opposite side of the political spectrum. His extensive tattoos and impressive beer belly gave some evidence of what he wanted to hear but before I could tell him what I thought he began an intense rant about "sending a girl to do a man's job." The moderates in this ongoing debate seemed to be few and far between.

People were usually disappointed when I answered their question about how women were performing on the job. The truth was I was never in a position to really know. There were fewer than 40 women out of a work force of about 10,000. I never worked with a female firefighter at an actual emergency incident until I became a chief. At that point I was supervising women who had been promoted to company officer positions. There was a huge difference in the physical demands of a firefighter and those of an officer. The firefighters did the brutally demanding hands-on work, the officers were supervisors, and while they had their own challenges to deal with, they were spared from the exhaustion of stretching hoses, forcing doors and overhauling buildings.

There was a lot of banter in the firehouse kitchen about certain women who were said to be incompetent or totally inappropriate for the job. I had no firsthand experience working with them but generalizations are almost always inaccurate. I believe there were some who were good firefighters but I also suspect that there were a few who should have never been hired.

I can say with certainty that when I became a chief and experienced working with female company officers their job performance was uniformly excellent. Shelia was one of my lieutenants. She worked in an active engine company in Manhattan and was everything I could ask for in a fire officer. Shelia was bright and motivated, an extremely good administrator, and most important, a very competent fireground supervisor. I never actually asked her but I often wondered how she felt being such a minority in a male-dominated department. I do know that if my own daughter wanted to be a firefighter (which, given the dangerous nature of the job, I am relieved to say she does not) I would hope for someone like Shelia to be a mentor for her.

Of course, in describing just a few individuals I am neglecting the dozens of others who also left such strong impressions. What may have appeared to be a homogenous mass of blue uniforms marching in a St. Patrick's Day parade was actually an eclectic group with wide-ranging skills and interests. They were hard-working, blue-collar people you would want on your side in a bar fight or in a dangerous situation. I've had jobs with coworkers who may have been more educated and perhaps spoke with less of a New York accent but I never worked with a group as capable of accomplishing so much under such trying conditions. And, at the risk of sounding like someone making an acceptance speech at the Oscars, nothing I ever accomplished as a chief would have been even remotely possible without the support they always gave me.

What's Behind
Door Number 2?

One of the hardest things I had to develop in my work was the ability to perceive some kind of order among the chaos of a firefighting operation. So much seemed to be going on at the same time. In New York City even a relatively simple fire would typically call for a response of at least nine companies and about 60 firefighters. The incessant, loud messages that blared out of the fireground radios were accompanied by the sound of personnel shouting urgent messages to each other. The background symphony was enhanced by the rumblings (and diesel smell) of all the fire trucks, the shattering windows, and panicky yells of the building residents. Fires are very noisy settings. If your rapidly pumping adrenaline didn't raise your blood pressure the work environment surely did.

The bombardment of fireground distractions made it especially difficult to see the "big picture" in a fire scenario. As a brand new firefighter I tended to be very task-oriented and narrow-minded in my approach to the work. Rather than viewing my role as a part of the general firefighting plan it was much easier, and less stressful, to concentrate on the hose I was operating or the particular tool I was using. No matter how many books I may have read about the importance of overall strategy there was a strong tendency to focus exclusively on the ladder I was climbing, the axe I was swinging, or the nozzle I was struggling to control.

Extinguishing a fire was not as simple as putting water on the hot stuff. There were a number of subtle aspects to the art and science of firefighting. Naturally, experience made the best teacher. When I was a brand new "nozzle man," for example, I initially put most of my effort into physically advancing the hose line and was less perceptive to the more hidden signs that might indicate an inadequate volume of water or insufficient ventilation of the fire area. Operating a 2½-inch diameter hose line was an extremely physical task. Kind of like squatting down on the floor and wrestling with an irritable anaconda while wearing 70 pounds of equipment. If I allowed myself to get too mentally involved in the physical battle I ran the risk of opening the nozzle at the wrong time or in the wrong place and potentially hurting other firefighters. The brute force that was required to perform the job added to the difficulty of being aware of my surroundings and seeing the ramifications of my fireground efforts.

Peer pressure also encouraged a nearsighted approach to the job. Acceptance by your coworkers can make or break your experience in the fire department. An aggressive display of your skills with the axe, power saw, or nozzle can be a means of showing your eagerness to be part of the "team" and your ability to contribute to the operation. Unfortunately, at times such activity can be overindulgent in muscle effort and somewhat lacking in the necessary mental preparation. Some of my worst bruises were not caused by the fire itself but by overly enthusiastic coworkers.

All of these factors tended to create a level of tunnel vision in any new firefighter. Regardless of the rank one may have eventually achieved or the number of years performed on the job most firefighters started their careers with this same perspective. And some embarrassing and enlightening moments often came with that perspective.

One cathartic moment occurred when I was a firefighter. Having initially worked in an engine company I decided to transfer to a ladder unit in order to diversify my knowledge. A ladder company performs the so-called "truck" skills at a fire. They are the ones who force open doors, vent windows, position ladders, and perform search and rescue operations. I wound up in a mid–Manhattan ladder company that did a lot of running and had a reputation for being really good at forcible entry.

The members of a ladder company, like any other group of people who work together, established their own pecking order. The unit officer would assign responsibilities to his five firefighters based on their aptitude and experience. As a new guy you could expect to be the "can man" for several months. Your job involved forcing your way through locked doors, initiating the search for victims and, if possible, using the heavy fire extinguisher you carried to knock down or contain the fire until the hose line was in position and ready to operate. I never minded being the low man on the truck totem pole. As the can man I had the opportunity to be right in the thick of the action, and since I was often crawling around inside the apartment before the hose was working, I learned how to approach and maneuver around the fire while it was still ripping. The extinguisher or "can" weighed about 30 pounds and after carrying it around for a long time I felt like my right arm was about three inches longer than my left.

As the unit officers got to know me better, and having served my apprenticeship as the can man, I eventually graduated to the forcible entry or "irons" position. At that point they knew me well enough to realize that I wasn't a total idiot who was likely to get myself or someone else killed and that I was starting to know my way around the fireground.

As the forcible entry guy I was the lead man in the process of forcing doors. Depending on the nature of the locking device, my array of equipment ranged from intricate metal picks to heavy steel tools that looked like something a Roman gladiator would carry. At times I also got to use a gas-powered saw to cut locks. I loved having the irons position. Each door was a different challenge and the task of forcing them open was a puzzle that had to be solved by a combination of mental analysis and physical skills. I always kept myself in good physical shape but at 170 pounds I lacked the girth and strength of some of the 250-pound behemoths I worked with. I was built more like a place kicker rather than a defensive tackle so I had to learn to take full mechanical advantage of the tools to do the job. I did once kick down a wooden door John Wayne–style but most of the time I had to really concentrate on the mechanisms and techniques involved.

So I was really excited about the prospect of catching a job when I started to get the irons position and eagerly awaited my first opportunity to do some damage to a door. I didn't have to wait long. Early on a night tour we responded as the first due truck for a fire in a store. At nighttime a commercial district in mid–Manhattan looked like an unwelcoming no man's land with only the occasional drunk or prostitute walking the empty sidewalks and a sporadic garbage or newspaper delivery truck roaring through the streets. It was midtown but a different side of midtown, kind of what you might expect to see in Cleveland, or Detroit, or a detective novel, and not what would be recommended viewing in a Fodor's guide to Manhattan. It felt remote and quiet, like the city was your own sanctuary and not the mass of humanity you experienced in the daytime. It was a slice of Manhattan I hadn't really seen before and I kind of liked it.

The buildings were heavily secured at night with heavy, steel roll-down gates held in position by a number of sturdy locks. It was possible to cut right through the roll-down gates but usually it was quicker and easier to cut off each of the individual locks. Once they were removed you could lift up the entire gate just like the store owner did when he returned every morning and create a large means of egress for fighting the fire.

As the fire burned in the store I watched the dark smoke push out through the seams of the store gate and realized that I had been presented with my first opportunity to actually use the forcible entry saw. That particular tool was the nosiest thing on the fireground. You would start it by pulling up on a cord much like a chainsaw only with considerably more heft. Instead of a toothed blade it rapidly spun a black abrasive disk

designed to grind its way through steel. It created both an intense decibel level and some of the most striking visual effects at a nighttime fire
scene. As the blade worked its way through a piece of metal it created a
comet-like trail of sparks that look like a Fourth of July fireworks display.
The secret to using it properly was to apply just the right amount of throt-
tle pressure while you kept an intense focus on the lock you were cutting.

This particular roll-down gate was secured by a number of heavy-duty
locks and my forcible entry partner and I immediately went to work. As
he held the first lock in position with a metal tool I revved up the saw and
started cutting. Sparks flew and within a minute that first lock was toast.

The remaining locks were more of a challenge. They were covered
by steel shields designed to make them harder to cut and were located at
positions that were awkward for us to work in. I was undeterred, and the
adrenaline-fueled battle of Man vs. Door continued.

The assault on the security gate went on for some time. Finally,
flushed with success, we rolled up the gate, stepped back, and for the first
time noticed that there had been a smaller door just to our right that had
apparently been much easier to open. The hose line was already stretched
through it and had knocked down much of the fire while we were deeply
entrenched in our personal campaign with the gate. I don't know if we

**Cutting a lock with the power saw always produces a loud, spectacular show
on the fireground (photograph by Bill Tompkins).**

were more surprised or embarrassed as we went inside to help search and overhaul the store.

Just about any senior firefighter you can get to be totally honest (which might be a challenge in itself) would admit to having some sort of experience like this. The lesson that always emerges is to slow down, observe, and think before you get immersed in a task. Even a "simple" forcible entry assignment requires a form of size-up prior to starting the work (take it from one who's been there).

This certainly carries over for stuff we do away from the fireground. I can think of the carpentry projects I've had to redo because I started cutting lengths of wood before I had sufficiently planned the job. Or consider how much safer it would be to drive a car if everyone maintained a broad perspective of the road rather than focusing too narrowly. And I won't even go into how cell phones have kept us from seeing (and ironically communicating with) the people around us.

An instructor once told me that there are no mistakes on the fireground, only learning opportunities. Forcing that store gate was just such an opportunity for me. My forcible entry partner and I never discussed our experience. But even when I eventually got promoted and became a chief responsible for managing large fires and emergencies I still felt the need to ask myself, "What perfectly obvious thing did I miss this time?"

Celebrity Steam Leaks

Manhattan was a very different place when I worked there as a fire-fighter in the 1980s. Women wore "big" hair and had discovered the body shaping magic of Spandex. They also dressed in garments with padded shoulders that gave them the profile of an NFL linebacker and created a "power look." (Though it should also be pointed out that they were not allowed to wear pants on the floor of the U.S. Senate until 1993.)

It was the era before the average price of an apartment reached one million dollars and the real estate market became somewhat dominated by foreign investors. You couldn't buy anything for $24 worth of wampum but the lower rents had hatched a variety of peep shows, sex clubs, and welfare hotels in midtown. Such occupancies spawned an eclectic mix of street people who mingled with the crowds of commuting office workers. They ranged from harmless poor people who were down on their luck to prostitutes and mentally deranged souls that you would go out of your way to avoid.

The AIDS crisis had begun but the partying was still going on. I once responded to a renowned sex club called Plato's Retreat for a mattress fire (I don't know if it was caused by a carelessly dropped cigarette or the result of some kind of erotic experiment). And when I drove home from work through the West Side I routinely saw guys cruising in cars with New Jersey plates seeking quick and inexpensive moments of instant romance and gratification from the streetwalkers.

For a while I befriended a street character called Sock Man. He was a young black guy who would resolutely stand in the middle of congested traffic on 8th Avenue selling plastic packages of sweat socks. I have no idea how he acquired them, and I never bought anything from him, but I kind of liked his entrepreneurial spirit. He would see me and yell, "Hey, fireman!" to which I would respond "My man, Sock Man!" In a previous life I think he may have been John Jacob Astor or Cornelius Vanderbilt.

The midtown skyline was pretty much the same as it looks today but back then many of the occupancies were different. Some gloomy and crowded welfare hotels were also crammed into that skyline. We had a couple of enormous old buildings in our response area that, in their time, had been very respectable hotels. Their time had long come and gone. The decorative masonry and intricate terra cotta features were still there but they were no longer offering the safe, comfortable rooms for tourists. Instead they had been transformed into wretched dumping grounds for people on welfare.

Someone must have earned a huge amount of money managing those places because the government dished out rents to house enormous numbers of welfare clients in them. The buildings were both profitable businesses and mini-ghettos and they had all of the issues that came with ghettos. The majority of the residents were just people struggling to get by. But the druggies, thieves, and habitual lowlifes that also stayed there made life miserable for the other residents, the neighborhood, and the firefighters.

We were called there on a regular basis for fires and false alarms. Most of the time it was for a routine mattress fire but occasionally we had a good job that would burn out a room or two and further displace the occupants. The fires always seemed to come at ridiculous hours in the middle of the night. And, as far as the activities going on in the street, there seemed to be no distinction between daytime and nighttime. At one o'clock in the morning you would see unsupervised kids playing in the lobby or on the sidewalks just a few feet removed from the ever-present prostitutes. I couldn't help but contrast their tough existence with my growing up years. I spent much of my childhood hanging out with friends on the streets of a drab, blue-collar Brooklyn neighborhood. But those streets were safe and we had stable homes and families and we grew up to be cops and firefighters and the occasional teacher or lawyer. The welfare urchins I saw didn't have a prayer of ever experiencing a normal or productive life. Oliver Twist would have fit right in their world.

The throng of unsavory characters that plagued midtown kept us really active most nights either for legitimate emergencies or annoying false alarms. Once an alarm came in around 4 a.m. during an especially busy tour. When we arrived at the building there was no sign of smoke or fire and a slightly disheveled-looking lady was calmly waiting for us on the front steps. Great, I thought, another lowlife bothering us for no reason. She said there was a steam leak in her apartment. Somewhat bleary-eyed we walked upstairs to discover that the relief valve had come off of her radiator. It took all of 10 seconds to shut the radiator and stop the leak. The woman thanked us profusely and explained that, being from California, she was not familiar with steam heat and was always taught to call the fire department for help. I remember noting how friendly and well-spoken she was. When we left the building our officer excitedly told us that the woman was Whoopi Goldberg. Unimpressed, I responded, "Who is Whoopi Goldberg? And how can she not know how to shut off a radiator valve?" (This must have been before she made it really big, or maybe I just wasn't watching a lot of comedy acts at the time.)

Occasionally I think of this incident when see Whoopi in a movie or on television. And I'm reminded of the lessons it reinforced. First, Whoopi *was* a nice person. Second, you have to be careful about the assumptions you make when you first see somebody. The big city is no doubt full of panhandlers, con men, and a multitude of other unpleasant sorts. But you never know when you might stumble upon a Whoopi or a Sock Man.

Going Down

If someone woke you up at 2 a.m. and asked you to draw a picture of a firehouse you would most likely kick them out of your bedroom and immediately reach for either your cell phone or your weapon, depending on your political bent or NRA membership. But if for some reason you chose to grab your pencils and start drawing, you would probably gather artistic inspiration from a number of sources. Childhood images from storybooks, cartoons, and television shows undoubtedly linger somewhere in the inner recesses of your brain. Subconscious memories of the firehouse on your street that you walked past hundreds of times but never really looked at may kick in. Snippets of movies you watched as an adult might influence your artwork, perhaps elements from that scene in *Pleasantville* where a group of clueless firefighters are patiently awaiting their next call to rescue a cat stuck in a tree.

Regardless of the source of your graphic inspiration, your drawing is guaranteed to include certain core elements. There would be a number of burly guys staged somewhere in the work, many of them sporting healthy mustaches. Their choice of garb might vary but there would no doubt be an ample sprinkling of red suspenders holding up their pants. The Dalmatian would naturally make his appearance somewhere in the scene. And last but not least, the sliding pole would be situated in the precise spot that would give a proper sense of perspective to the entire drawing.

The firehouse sliding pole seems as American as apple pie. (And apparently as British as tea and clotted cream. Remember that unflattering view of Renee Zellweger sliding a pole in *Bridget Jones Diary*?) It's hard to picture a firehouse without one. The thought of a firefighter sliding down a pole is an image that combines excitement, fun, fascination, and danger all at the same time. However, most people's familiarity with poles is limited to what they retained from watching ancient episodes of the *Batman* television series. Let's face it, you are never going to see a pole in your home or place of business. The real estate lawyer working on the tenth floor of your office is not about to instantly slide down to the tax shelter department on the ninth floor to arrive in time for an important meeting. (Though it must be said that Anderson Cooper lives in an old renovated firehouse in New York City that still has one of the original poles. I have an image of him rapidly sliding down to scoop a story for CNN.)

Questions about sliding down a metal pole always came up when I told people I was a firefighter. They often seemed interested or amused by an act that I had performed so many times that I seldom really thought about it. It was just a small part of my job that I kind of took for granted. However, if I do pause to examine it, the act and the art of pole sliding was a rather cool experience. I got to slide my first pole when I was about 11 years old. I remember looking down the pole hole opening on the second floor of my father's firehouse and seeing his reassuring face standing at the bottom some 20 feet below me. I cautiously reached out and wrapped my arms and legs around the slick, polished brass. And I can still sense the boyish enthusiasm I felt as I slowly descended from what seemed like an enormous height.

The view from the top of a sliding pole. As an 11-year-old it seemed like a long way down (photograph by the author).

The officer on duty would probably not have been thrilled to know that a kid was sliding one of the poles in his firehouse. If I had been hurt he would have faced an enormous amount of paperwork along with the awkward challenge of explaining why an 11-year-old had even been engaged in such an activity. But sliding down that pole provided a sense of excitement that easily rivaled any of the mediocre athletic or academic accomplishments I had attained up to that point in my life. Little did I know that more than 50 years later I would still be sliding down poles and still enjoying it.

In reality the pole is less a cultural icon and more

a practical tool. Seconds counted in my profession. Time was of the essence for medical calls. Flame spread at a geometric rate in building fires. If a firefighter's response time was shortened by just a few seconds it could literally mean the difference between someone living or dying. The pole is a tool that has been around for a long time. Like many practical developments it sprang from the creative skills of a single individual, someone who was able to view the obvious, see the need for change, and innovate a unique solution. In 1878 David Kenyon's moment had arrived. He was a captain working in a three-story Chicago firehouse. Back then the feed for the horses was regularly delivered by a wagon that had a long wooden pole placed on top of the hay to keep it from falling off. When the wagon arrived at the firehouse both the hay and the wooden pole were stored on the top floor of the building. After David observed a firefighter using the pole to rapidly slide down when a fire alarm came in, he decided to build a permanent installation and he had a hole cut in the floor. The sliding pole had been officially invented and a tradition had started. Within two years the first brass pole was installed by the Boston Fire Department followed by other departments throughout the country. It was a natural fit since most fire stations were two or three stories high and David's simple concept quickly replaced the spiral staircases and sliding chutes that were previously used. I don't know if he filed for a patent or if he made any money from his invention but I think it's kind of sad that the device wasn't named for him. If life were fair we would have been sliding down the "Kenyon" rather than the pole for the past 140 years.

However you want to label it, a pole is a device that requires some training to properly master. The act of sliding is a step-by-step process that, over time, becomes just one fluid motion requiring no conscious thought, rather like riding a bicycle. Step one is to pull back the hinged, horizontal pole guard that's placed to keep anyone from accidentally falling down the hole in the floor. Next, you grab the pole with both hands and wrap your legs around it, keeping the outside of your left ankle flush against the pole. The pole guard snaps back into position behind you and creates a definitive sound informing you that there is no turning back, you are now committed to the slide. As you cling to the pole you adjust your rate of descent by the pressure of your hand grip. The speed can range from a slow, casual descent suitable for a visit to the kitchen to a swift plunge geared for an emergency response when you know you are the first due unit for a fire. The act of landing is the final and most crucial aspect of the slide. Here lies the greatest potential for injury, sprained ankles, most commonly. The feet of an experienced pole artist will contact the floor pads located at the bottom of the pole with just enough momentum to gently touch down followed by a graceful step away from the pole to avoid being hit by the next slider.

A true sliding guru is capable of coming to a complete stop at any position on the pole if, let's say, he happened to want a perspective of what life looked like midway between two floors. On the other hand, the pole novitiate fresh from a shower might be guilty of making an error like sliding with wet hands, which will produce a screeching sound that can be as irritating to the hands as it is to the ears. After hundreds of slides one reaches a comfort level that makes it all seem natural. I don't think anyone has ever actually slid while asleep but I often recall being abruptly awoken from a deep sleep in the bunk room and suddenly mounting the fire truck on the floor below with absolutely no memory of having been on the pole at all.

The type of pole you encountered varied as you traveled to different firehouses. My favorite, and the most common, was the traditional pole made of polished brass. It combined classic decor with a slick surface that allowed for a great hand grip and a readily controlled descent. The pole also wobbled a bit as you went down which added to the overall experience.

The classic brass sliding pole with guard rail (photograph by the author).

Some of the more modern firehouses had stainless steel poles. These just didn't look as good and had a significantly different feel. The wider diameter of the pole combined with the harsher steel surface gave them a sort of industrial feel. There's something to be said about the spirit of a material. Brass seemed to have a soul while stainless steel was kind of sterile. Also, there was no give and no wobble at all when you slid down a steel pole unlike the brass ones which moved and "interacted" with your body as you descended. It was as though the brass welcomed your embrace while the steel just briefly tolerated your presence.

At one point there were a few poles around

that had a mechanically activated metal shield positioned beneath the pole hole opening. The shield would snap open like a clamshell just before you slid down and just as quickly slam shut behind you once you passed through. It was designed to contain the diesel fumes produced by the trucks on the first floor. Sliding down those poles was kind of strange and conjured up vague images of the birth process as you were delivered from floor to floor through a yielding orifice. Fortunately, this type of pole was short-lived. Eventually adequate ventilation systems were installed that provided for cleaner air throughout the firehouse and granted a respite from the awkward experience of using such devices. After all, sliding should be a practical and enjoyable process and not the source of psychological analysis.

The ultimate pole experience was to be found in three-story firehouses. In those buildings you could instantly transport yourself from the gymnasium and locker room environment of the top floor through the dark, comforting world of the second-floor bunk room to the heavy truck garage on the first floor, all in a matter of seconds that bypassed the time-consuming use of two long stairways. I had a preference too for the older firehouses because it seemed like they had higher ceilings. For a brief time I worked in an engine company on the Lower East Side that had the longest sliding poles in the city. Twenty-eight feet may not be a world record but it sure felt like it when you were going down.

In retrospect, regardless of the type of pole, the act of sliding can be construed to have had a significance that ran much deeper than the mere act of rapid movement between floors. Much like Captain James Kirk being electronically transported from the Starship *Enterprise* it was a sort of symbolic physical and psychic leap of faith into the next, yet-to-be-experienced moments of your existence that awaited you on the floor below. And those moments could range from savoring a delicious meal in the comfort of a raucous firehouse kitchen to crawling blindly through a smoke-filled room, desperately trying to find your way out of a burning building.

Unfortunately, there are those who want to bring the era of the sliding pole to an end. For some time there has been an ongoing debate regarding the safety and future practicality of fire house poles. Pole opponents cite factors such as sliding injuries as a reason for eliminating them along with the potential for spreading diesel exhaust to the firefighters' living quarters. In addition, they highlight budgetary concerns arising from insurance expenses combined with enormous installation costs. As an example, two poles were installed not long ago in Seattle at a cost of $150,000 *each.*

On the other hand, pole supporters can point to the dramatically improved ventilation systems that are now standard in most firehouses.

When I first entered the FDNY there were no air circulation devices and it was just kind of accepted that the diesel fumes would eventually work their way out of the building on their own. Most of the television screens on the floor above were so covered with soot you could write your name on them. That is not the case now since the truck exhaust is hooked up to a hose and sucked out of the firehouse on every response.

Proponents of the pole can also cite the time-saving aspect of sliding down as opposed to using the stairs. I've seen various studies that indicate a range of five to 25 seconds in reduced response time. And with tight, expensive real estate markets in most urban areas the multi-story firehouse is likely to remain commonplace. But the fiercest pole defenders draw their support simply from the long-standing tradition of the sliding pole. Firefighters are some of the most conservative people you will encounter and they do not easily surrender their core values and customs.

It remains to be seen what the ultimate fate of the sliding pole will be. But it is at least possible that it might eventually go the way of the ice truck or the manual typewriter. If they are to disappear altogether you might want to make some room on your bucket list to slide down at least one time. It may not have the excitement or pizazz of skydiving or wind surfing but does have a definite physical appeal. Perhaps you can befriend a firefighter and coerce him into letting you try it. Or better yet, see if you can finagle yourself onto the guest list for Anderson Cooper's next party. As for me, it's a part of my job that I still kind of miss. And if I someday happen to come into some big money I will have to at least entertain the thought of installing one in my home.

Hey Lieu!

One of the great things about being in the FDNY was that I could pretty much carve out the kind of work that I wanted to do. I was initially assigned to an engine company and experienced the thrill of operating the business end of a working hose line. It was kind of amazing to see how it could instantly convert a room full of fire into a maelstrom of steam and white smoke. Then I got to perform the so-called "truck" tasks in a ladder company and learned how to search for victims, force my way through intricately locked doors, and use the science and techniques of air movement to vent a burning building. There was a great deal to absorb and all that was required was patience and the willingness to learn. And you could learn much in New York by working at various assignments in different areas of the city. There was no one, set-in-place career path in the FDNY but rather a number of different routes to follow depending on your interests.

The same held true for promotions in the job. I could have been a firefighter for my entire career or chosen to pursue the road of increasingly competitive civil service promotional exams. Successful completion of those tests first led to a position as a company officer responsible for supervising one unit and eventually a job as a chief who commanded many units. Many of my coworkers chose to remain at the firefighter rank either because they loved the hands-on aspect of the work or they didn't have the time to study for promotion because they were working a side job or had childcare responsibilities at home.

Although I really liked many of the physical aspects of working as a firefighter I made the decision early on to study for promotion. I was motivated by a number of reasons. While the work was stimulating it was also exhausting and I didn't envision walking up five flights of stairs and pounding down a door when I was 55 years old (though I did marvel at the sight of a few rare firefighters who were still efficiently functioning into their 60s). Also, though I was well paid as a New York City firefighter, a promotion would lead to a higher salary with a subsequently increased pension income.

However, of all the legitimate reasons for seeking to move up in the organization nothing motivated me more than the fact that I was interested in learning all I could about the job. And that meant experiencing the work at the supervisory level. Ironically, when you got promoted in the fire department your job got even more dangerous and difficult. A company officer was no longer humping tools and performing the physical work but he was expected to be the first one inside a burning building to instantly size up the dangers, initiate a strategy, and ensure the safety of his men. In all honesty it was not a role I comfortably envisioned myself being in. But like so much else in my career, and in my life, the things that I feared always lingered in the back of my mind and tempted me to pursue them. The fear of missing out on something good usually won out over any limiting neuroses my psyche tended to cling to.

So for a number of years I immersed myself in the process of studying for the lieutenant's exam. I spent countless hours tucked away in the comfort of my home or in the discomfort of a firehouse basement studying an endless list of firefighting techniques, building construction details, laws, and administrative procedures. The HBO movies that had previously accompanied me during my long and lonely middle of the night duties at the house watch desk were replaced by the obsessive yellow highlighting I used to break down and memorize a massive amount of technical material. It seemed like an endless process but I attacked it with the intensity of an Ebenezer Scrooge staring at his ledgers or a Talmudic scholar driven by seven cups of coffee.

My realistic goal was just to be promoted one time and become a company officer. Given the Herculean effort involved in studying I couldn't imagine that over a period of several years I would successfully hurdle four promotional exams and eventually become a deputy chief. When my first lieutenant's exam was thrown out because of an alleged cheating scandal I continued to work and prepare for the next one. I did just as well on that test and, with six years on the job, I achieved the rank of lieutenant. For the first time in my work life I was going to be a supervisor, the guy who had to lead and occasionally crack the whip, the person who would no longer answer to "Tom" but to "Lieu" when someone wanted my attention (not to be confused with the "loo" of British verbiage which refers to the bathroom, a fact that most firefighters were thankfully unaware of).

By FDNY standards six years was very little time for a lieutenant to have on the job. It added to the challenge since I could expect to be supervising a lot of firefighters who had more experience in the department than I did. I did not feel at all ready for the position, but then again I probably didn't really feel prepared for any of the promotions I eventually reached. Each time I kind of grew into the rank. I wasn't promoted because I was brilliant or the best firefighter around; I just had the persistence and drive that was rewarded by the civil service system.

Most firefighters are plagued by some doubts before taking the big leap from being a firefighter riding in the back of the rig to becoming the officer in charge sitting up front. The two biggest jumps in responsibility in the FDNY were from the rank of firefighter to lieutenant and from captain to chief. Just a few days before my first tour as a lieutenant a very competent firefighter I worked with told me that he would have to get high if he had to perform in the rank I was about to assume. I'm not sure if he was serious, or what his choice of intoxicant would have been, but it certainly showed his discomfort with even the thought of being promoted (he eventually became a very competent, and sober, lieutenant himself).

I was assigned to the Bronx on the day I was promoted. This was not only going to be a dramatic change in job duties but also a new work environment that was radically different from the mid–Manhattan world I had experienced as a firefighter. It seemed like any incident that occurred in Manhattan affected large numbers of people, took a long time to resolve, and received enormous media attention. The Bronx on the other hand was an "out there" kind of place that had significantly more fire activity than most parts of the city. Both the borough and its firefighters still carried the outlaw reputation that grew from the 1960s when entire city blocks became an apocalyptic jumble of devastated, burnt-out buildings. It was no longer the 60s but there were still some tough neighborhoods plagued by drugs, arson, and the not-so-occasional gunshot.

The Bronx had its own ethos. If Manhattan was the city's central nervous system the Bronx was its soul, or, in certain areas, its armpit. Bronx buildings were drabber-looking and the fires more frequent but working there meant more than facing new fire challenges. It was also a different culture. Some sections were home to a core of lowlifes who shot up drugs, the borough's reputation, and each other. But the majority of residents were decent people who commuted to their jobs and enjoyed what pleasures were to be had. Working in Manhattan I had experienced traffic-clogged streets that were extremely loud in the daytime but became quiet and subdued at night when midtown seemed to shut down. That's when the Bronx was just waking up, especially in the summer. Entire families would escape from their hot tenements to congregate on the sidewalks and dance to loud music spewing from enormous speakers perched on rusty fire escapes. The neighborhoods were accented by Salsa and beer and on Saturdays the party went on all night. I have met some out-of-towners who visited the Bronx Zoo and told me they felt like they were in a foreign country. After working there for years I viewed it differently. The Bronx was its own thing but it was most definitely a slice of America. To many who lived there mid–Manhattan was the foreign nation.

Once I became a lieutenant I was no longer "one of the boys" but a supposed leader of men, someone who could earn obedience and respect from subordinates while at the same time maintain the necessary distance required of a leader. It was a position that took some getting used to. Back then there was no training for the job. On a Friday I worked my last tour as a firefighter in a Manhattan ladder company. Two nights later I was working my first tour as a company officer in a Brooklyn engine company. To say that I was a bit nervous would be an understatement. I was pretty comfortable with the firefighting aspect of the job but the leadership part was new to me.

Wherever you worked in the city there were certain management skills that a new lieutenant had to master. I had never been a great believer in the numerous management/leadership books that circulate about with their "shortcuts to success," "50 leadership lessons from George Patton," and "taking charge of yourself" themes. I much preferred to learn on my own using basic intelligence along with a hands-on knowledge of what it took to lead and motivate people. It came down to being liked and re-spected at the same time and I was usually well-liked wherever I worked. The keeping your distance as a leader part came easily to me since I was pretty much a loner to begin with.

One of the hardest things to initially develop was the ability to simply say "No." Someone new to a supervisory role really wants to be liked and accepted by his subordinates so there is a natural desire to want to please them. The vast majority of firefighters who worked for me were very sup-portive and I seldom had to ask twice to get something accomplished. However, there was the occasional "square rooter" who always seemed to have an angle and had no limit to the extent of a favor they would re-quest of me, regardless of how awkward a position it would put me in as the unit officer. Things like wanting their 10-year-old to ride with us on the rig when we responded to an alarm. Or wanting to take the engine "just outside the city" to buy a piece of hardware they needed for a home improvement project (which would leave you know who to explain why an FDNY fire truck happened to be involved in an accident out of the city limits). But the most unusual request I ever got was from someone I that really enjoyed working with who wanted my permission to leave work and go home because he was distraught over the death of his dog. I have no doubt that he was upset but the department bereavement leave policy was designed for immediately relieving on-duty personnel in the event of a death of a *human* family member and, of course, I said no.

After being confronted by several such requests I began to develop the art and technique of making no decision at all. This was not a management tool found in any textbook. And it could not be used on the fireground where life-and-death decisions were made and instant compliance with an order would affect the safety of both civilians and firefighters. But I found that inside the firehouse, if I could put certain requests on hold for just a few minutes, it would allow me enough time to think how comfortable I really was with allowing the requested favor. And, just as in fighting a fire, it was a good rule of thumb to listen to my gut reaction. If something felt bad it *was* bad.

Like many green, inexperienced lieutenants I was often carried by my men through periods of unfamiliarity with the job. They were excellent at what they did and shared their knowledge about the intricacies of the buildings in their response areas. This really helped when I was assigned to work in a neighborhood I had never been to before. Firefighting procedures are standard throughout all sections of New York City but it was tough coming into a company with no idea of the peculiarities of the district or of the firefighters I would be working with. They knew that I was in the middle of an enormous transition and learning process and they always stepped up to help me through the rough spots. Firefighters tend to be a raucous group and when I was working in my office I could often hear the loud humor and boisterous activity that was happening on the floor below. I would crank out my paperwork until the meal was ready and announced by the ringing of a loud bell or by a guy yelling up the pole hole, "Hey Lieu, it's on the table!" It was somewhat like supervising a crew of pirates only these pirates could be relied on if I needed something accomplished in the firehouse or to perform emergency work on the fireground.

After a number of routine responses my first really good job as a lieutenant finally came one night while I was working in a Bronx ladder company. An apartment on an upper floor of a six-story building was on fire and I was the first ladder unit on the scene. When the battalion chief saw me in the lobby he said I had a "job" upstairs but he said it so calmly it was obvious that this was just another incident for him in a long career of fires. I remember wondering how he could be so calm when I felt so on edge. As the engine began stretching the hose line I started walking up the stairs knowing that my forcible entry team and I were going to be the first firefighters to reach the burning apartment. That meant forcing a door, confronting the fire with no hose line in place, and making a quick evaluation of the possibility of entering to make a search for victims before we had water to contain the flames. You wanted to be aggressive, especially in an occupied residence at night, but you didn't want to do anything stupid and get your men hurt.

I had walked up a lot of stairs when I was a firefighter but this was different. I still felt a bit naked just carrying an officer's light instead of the heavy tools that my men were burdened with. For the first time I was heading to a fire as a leader rather than a follower and I knew that I had to at least look the part. One of the things that helped me as I moved up through the ranks of the fire department was that I was never one to wear my heart on my sleeve. I was basically a very calm person and it was usually hard to look at me and figure out exactly what I might be thinking or feeling. Scared, excited, bored, happy or sad, I tended not to project much, a characteristic that had undoubtedly confused and frustrated a number of women in previous short-lived relationships. But having this kind of persona was an advantage as a fire officer. Nobody wanted to work for a leader who got visibly angry and yelled at a fire. And no one felt confident working if the man in charge projected discomfort or fear. I was a pretty good actor and at this first attempt at being a leader I suppressed the uneasiness I felt and tried to deliver the right lines.

As we headed up the stairs I told my men to pace themselves. They were facing a climb of several flights and would probably have to force open the door to the apartment. Walking up numerous steps while wearing fire gear and carrying heavy tools was an onerous task and their work was just going to be starting once they got up there. Apartment doors tended to be heavily secured in the Bronx and it was often difficult to overcome the initial hurdle of forcing your way inside. That task would be immediately followed by crawling through several rooms to search for victims along with the exhausting window smashing and demolition tasks that ladder companies perform.

It seemed like it was all over very quickly. And as far as fires go this one went very well. Thankfully there were no victims and the fire was contained to one room. It turned out to be exactly the kind of routine job I needed to break myself in as a "leader of men." Not that the quality of my leadership had any influence at all on the operation. My firefighters knew what had to be done and they had accomplished it well. When we were back in the firehouse one of my guys came up to me and said, "Lieu, you were right on with that call." I had absolutely no idea what he was talking about and didn't remember making any significant "calls" at all at the job. It turned out that he was referring to the calm instruction I had given them to pace themselves as they climbed up to the fire. I had apparently pulled it off. The acting had worked. I had performed in the way I thought a company officer *should* behave, the same way I had seen many competent officers handle themselves when I had worked under their leadership as a firefighter. I guess that sometimes it's not how you feel that counts, it's how you look.

A few weeks later I wasn't exactly sure what to feel when I worked a night tour out in Queens. It was a neighborhood where second- and third-generation Irish residents clung tenaciously to their distant heritage by cavorting in the Gallic-themed pubs and restaurants. If you liked the color green and had any affiliation with Saint Patrick this was the place to be. It contrasted sharply from my normal Bronx work world, and even though I looked like someone who would fit right in, I kind of felt like an outsider.

Usually I could get a sense of what an individual firehouse was like the moment I walked through the door. This one seemed clean and organized but it didn't look like it had a lot of fire activity, kind of what I expected given the nature of the area. What I hadn't anticipated was the age level of the firefighters I would be supervising. I was accustomed to working with very young guys who were attracted to the more active fire areas of the city. Here I was met by a group of gray-haired veterans who had clearly been on the job for decades and were approaching retirement. I wondered if my brief six-year firefighting background was enough to prepare for this. How exactly was I going to "lead" men who were years senior to me in both age and experience?

Of all the guys working that night two in particular stood out. They were in their 60s, white-haired, Irish-looking, and somewhat deaf. Forget about working with your father—this was like working with both of your grandfathers. Each of them must have had 40 years on the job which gave them a combined 74 more years in the department than I had. And it looked like they had worked many of those years in the same firehouse although all that time spent with each other had not led to any kind of compatible working relationship. They related more like an elderly couple in a marriage that had gone bad about 20 years ago and spent much of the evening bitching and moaning at each other in a loud dialogue that was amplified by hearing loss. Even the supper that night was old school. Gone were the salads and garlic flavored pastas I enjoyed in the Bronx. These guys wanted the dry roast beef, frozen string beans, and mashed potatoes they had been eating since the 1940s.

Fortunately there was generally a persistent adherence to the chain of command in the FDNY. Even though these old-timers had so much more of a fire background than I did they treated me kindly and with respect. They reserved their vitriol for each other as in "Walsh, pass those fuckin' potatoes before you die of a heart attack," which elicited a response like "Just wait your turn, you shanty Irish bastard." The more time I spent with them the more I liked them and the entertainment they provided.

We did get a job that night. Around two o'clock in the morning we responded to a fire in an apartment building. It was a typical one room, one hose line fire that went well and was handled quickly. I remember less about the fire and more about the actions of my two ancient grandfathers. They stretched the hose line for what must have been the nine hundredth time in their careers and displayed a synchrony in their work that was in complete contrast with their combative day to day interactions. It was a pleasure to watch the ease and professionalism that reflected decades of firefighting experience. And it was even more of a pleasure to hear a high volume "Walsh, get your Irish ass up here and help me with this fuckin' hose" as I headed up the stairs.

I spent nine years as a company officer prior to becoming a chief, six of them as a lieutenant and three as a captain. Over that time I went to a lot of fires, wore out several cars in my commute to work, got married, and had my first child. Both my work world and private life had changed. And I had changed too. I was much removed from the shy person who questioned his abilities and felt more like someone who was comfortable giving orders. And I knew that those orders would be complied with if I showed integrity and concern for my people. When I heard someone yell, "Hey Lieu!" I no longer felt like an impostor playing the role of boss. Instead I had assumed the role of a competent fire officer and first line supervisor in the New York City Fire Department, a role that would lead to seeing some memorable sights and meeting some interesting people.

Buffs

I'm really not much of a poetry connoisseur but a line from a Robert Service poem has stuck with me: "There's a race of men that don't fit in." The poem is about men who go through life like rolling stones, always looking for the next big adventure or experience and ignoring the predictable paths of those around them. Whenever I think of that line it seems to conjure up the image of the fire buff. A "buff" is a guy who is not a firefighter but has an intense interest in the fire department and all things connected to it. The term itself has fire service roots and derives from the buffalo-skin coats worn by firefighters in the 19th century.

There may be a few female buffs somewhere out there but I have never met one. In my experience they have all been men. Their ages, personalities, and backgrounds may vary but they all share the same interests. They follow a passion for firefighting, fire equipment, and fire lore with the same enthusiasm as a rabid Yankee fan who can rattle off the names of obscure players or esoteric baseball statistics.

I am unsure of the source of their fire fascinations but then again where do any of our preferences stem from? Perhaps it's just in our DNA. Some buffs were frustrated firefighters who were unable to pursue that career path because of medical issues or for other practical reasons. Others had very successful professions (including at least one doctor that I am aware of) but had a need to immerse themselves in a work culture that was totally different, much like Robert Service's race of men.

I always felt somewhat ambivalent toward buffs. The vast majority of them were likable, decent people. A few were annoying to be around and some were outright nerdy. Some were extremely intelligent, one was mentally challenged. And while there were buffs I really enjoyed conversing with there were others I couldn't wait to get away from. But they always treated me with respect and I tried to do likewise.

They liked to watch fires. Observing a firefighting operation was sort of their version of going to the Super Bowl. And I had no problem with that with the exception of one buff in particular who had a habit of bombarding me with questions as I was trying to command an incident. Usually one of my men would step up and gently guide him away to shield me from the distraction. However, for the most part buffs kept their distance on the fireground and allowed us the space we needed to do our work. They always supported firefighters and could be counted on if you needed a favor like picking up a soda or a pack of cigarettes.

The only aspect of buffing I could never make peace with was the vicarious excitement that some of them seemed to enjoy at a fire scene. Even though it wasn't their intention to see people get hurt the essence of their hobby involved watching bad stuff happen. To me the fire was my job. I worried about the safety of my men and the residents of the building. The fact that the scene may have been visually spectacular meant nothing. I just wanted to get it safely under control and move on to the next fire. After many years and hundreds of fires I was ok with a tour in which nothing happened. I got really good at managing an incident but I never lost sight of the fact that you were only as good as your last fire and there was no guarantee that all would survive the next one. On the other hand, some buffs were very disappointed if a fire didn't occur. Kind of like the motivated journalist embedded in an infantry platoon who can't wait to see some combat so he can report on it. One buff once told me that he was hoping for sleep deprivation when he hung out in the firehouse for a tour, meaning that he would get to observe a busy night. How nice for you, I thought. You get some thrills while my men and I get our asses kicked and someone loses their home or business, or possibly even their life.

So while many of the buffs were good guys on some level I kind of viewed them as somewhat eccentric characters who followed the job in the way that a pilot fish would shadow a shark. They enjoyed hanging around the firehouse and in some cases went to visit the same company for years. On a pure "seniority" basis they often had a lot more time with the unit than many of the younger firefighters and were informally accepted as being a part of the firehouse even though they had no official capacity. Sort of like if you had a guy in your office who wasn't an employee of your firm but liked hanging out with the accounts receivable department and regaling them with stories about the time when the big Smothers account refused to pay up back in the crash of 2008. Though I guess when you come right down to it their fascinations were no more esoteric or nerdy than, say, my interest in reading about naval history or following New York Giants trivia. The big difference is that I have no interest in hanging out with sailors or sitting in the Giants locker room, especially after a game when it probably smells rather foul.

Of all the buffs I met over the years a few are especially memorable. I met Bobby in the Bronx. Bobby was a gentle soul who had wrapped his life around the fire department and found a home away from home in a firehouse that was located a few blocks from his apartment. He was afflicted with a form of autism that didn't allow him to engage in normal conversations but gave him a remarkable ability to remember amazingly detailed bits of information. Picture Dustin Hoffman's character in the movie *Rain Man* and you get a sense of what he was like.

I was a relatively new lieutenant when I first arrived to work a day tour at Bobby's company. As I was walking toward the firehouse Bobby came out to meet me and asked me for my name. I was a bit taken aback since I knew he wasn't a firefighter and it seemed an odd request from a civilian on the street. I told him who I was and he immediately regaled me with a dazzling burst of facts and information about me and my career. He knew the exact date I had been promoted to lieutenant. He knew my badge number. He even knew what the weather had been like on my promotion date. It was as if he had my personnel folder wide open in front of him and he excitedly and rapidly continued his nonstop monologue. Initially I felt shocked and somewhat assaulted by his possession of what to me was personal information. But I quickly recognized his affliction, gave him a few polite nods and continued on into the firehouse.

As I got to spend more time with Bobby my amazement at his capacity for trivia was soon replaced by an appreciation of how well he fit in despite his disability. The guys in the firehouse really seemed to care for his well-being and were always willing to extend themselves to help him. Bobby in turn was immersed in the world that he loved and obsessed with. It was kind of nice to see his child-like enthusiasm for the fire department. It was even nicer to see that being in the company provided him with a daily focus in his life.

I haven't been to that firehouse for some time but I hope that Bobby is still there. He was never going to have a normal life but he had found his niche in this world. It was a great example of a buff who was good for a firehouse and a firehouse that was good for a buff.

When I was a firefighter in Manhattan I worked in a company that was home to the Babe Ruth of fire buffs. Matty had hung out in the unit for decades. I don't know for sure just when he started visiting but I wouldn't be surprised if at some point in his youth he had helped feed the horses. I first met him when I had just transferred in and was new to the company. Early one evening I was assigned to the house watch desk which meant answering the phones, receiving the alarms, and generally keeping an eye on all the equipment and security of the firehouse. However, no one mentioned that there was a long-standing buff who always visited. So I was quite taken aback when an old man well into his 80s and formally dressed in a suit suddenly materialized in front of me at the house watch desk. He briefly nodded as he walked past and continued to casually walk toward the kitchen area in the rear of the firehouse. He moved very slowly with the assistance of a cane but at the same time appeared very relaxed, almost like he was walking through his own living room instead of a firehouse.

Matty's sudden appearance was kind of bizarre—in fact, I would have been less shocked if a well-built woman in a thong had suddenly appeared in the firehouse (especially since the neighborhood had an entourage of streetwalkers). But there was something about the way he carried himself that kept me from snapping "Who the hell are you and where do you think you're going?" So I just allowed him to proceed on into the inner sanctum of the firehouse despite some discomfort on my part since I was acting as the security guard of the place. However, in letting him go past I spared myself what could have been a pretty embarrassing experience. Imagine me, the new guy assigned to the company for just a few days, blocking an elderly man from entering the firehouse when that man had been a beloved visitor for decades before my arrival? Another example in just listening to your gut to come up with the best decision, a lesson that would be reinforced over and over again throughout my career.

Matty was a walking encyclopedia of firefighting lore. He knew the location of most of the alarm boxes in mid–Manhattan and had met generations of firefighters. Despite his advanced age he still walked to the firehouse most evenings to have supper with us. He always sat in the same chair and would slowly eat his meal until the firehouse radio announced that a multiple alarm was occurring somewhere in the city. Whenever that happened he would immediately stop, grab a pencil, and with his gnarled, arthritic fingers write down the time, box number, and location of the fire. To me it seemed kind of obsessive but it was a routine he had followed for decades.

It was impossible not to like Matty. It was kind of like having a kindly grandfather hanging out in the firehouse. He had a sense of humor and could hold his own under a barrage of tough firehouse jesting. Beneath all the razzing, which had to be done in high volume because he was hard of hearing, you sensed that the guys had a genuine affection for him. He lived in a hotel down the block and at the end of the evening one or two firefighters would always walk him home to make sure he got there safely.

Matty was a sort of icon in the fire service. But beyond that I like to think of him as one of the many unknown New York residents who make the city an interesting place. He was a true Manhattanite who lived in the same place and wandered the same neighborhoods for years. He even had a Manhattan kind of fate. Despite his age he continued to walk the streets until he got knocked down in an encounter with a bicyclist and wound up in the hospital. Once he was there, as often happens with elderly people, complications set in and he died.

We held the equivalent of a department funeral for him and a large turnout of firefighters, officers, and chiefs showed up to pay their respects to a long-respected friend. Of all the buffs I met through the years I got to know Matty the best and enjoyed his company the most. It saddens me to think that there are guys now working in that firehouse who would have absolutely no idea who he was or even that he had ever been there. Then again, is that not the ultimate fate of all of us?

Bobby and Matty are good examples of buffs who managed to slide into comfortable, welcoming slots in the FDNY. However, I met one who tried to fake his way in. Fred (that's not his name) was actually a good guy. He appeared one day in our firehouse claiming to be a firefighter from Brooklyn who was temporarily assigned to an administrative assignment because of an injury. The story went that he hurt his shoulder in a building collapse and he couldn't wait to fully recover and get back to his firehouse. And quite a shoulder it was. He was about average height but extremely muscular and he often worked out with the other guys in the basement weight room. He looked and acted like a typical firefighter, was always friendly, and occasionally went out drinking with the guys. Over a period of weeks he ate meals with us, talked quite a bit about his fire experience and became a part of the house.

Like any other large institution there is an informal grapevine in the FDNY that manages to disseminate information throughout the job. If a guy screws up in Staten Island within hours they will be talking about it in the Bronx. After a while some of the things Fred was saying just didn't seem right and a few guys started getting suspicious. Someone made a phone call to the Brooklyn company he claimed to be from and they had never heard of him.

It turned out that Fred had wanted to become a firefighter but, despite his intimidating physique, he had a medical condition that barred him from getting the job. He left a handwritten letter on the kitchen poster board confessing that he had been living a lie with us and explaining why he did it. Very much like that "race of men" that Robert Service wrote about, he was constantly in pursuit of an experience that proved to be an unreachable goal. And rather than accepting that fact he tried to live a dishonest fantasy. It was so important for him to be a firefighter that his fantasy overcame his reality. I don't know if I was more surprised by his deception or saddened by his desperation. I wished I could have sat down and told him that he was basically a decent person and that if he had only been honest with us I'm sure we would have accepted him for who he was. Fred was a would-be firefighter who would have made a great buff. But sadly he was like a tragic figure in a play, always pursuing but never living up to his self-image.

I think that there is a bit of the buff in all of us. What child, or adult, for that matter, has not at some time been thrilled by the sight of a fire engine roaring by with the lights flashing and the siren screaming? Or gazed with curiosity through the open firehouse doors at the shining rigs, brass poles, and long racks of smoke-stained helmets and coats? Kurt Vonnegut once wrote that a fire truck was the most visible symbol of man's humanity to man. If you happen to see one of those symbols drive by, and you can identify it as being an engine or a ladder unit, and you can describe its specific function at a fire, you may be bordering on the cusp of being a buff. If you know the engine's pumping capacity, the number of runs it had last year, and maybe even the date it went into service, you are no doubt a full-fledged, end stage buff. And while I may not understand you I certainly salute your enthusiasm.

What If?

It's not always the most productive thing to do but there are often times when I can't help but indulge in the "what ifs" of life. Such escapist moments provide brief, tantalizing images of what might have been in alternate life scenarios. Questions and fantasies abound. What would have happened if I had moved to Colorado when I was young? Which failed relationships could have succeeded had I been more receptive to them? Were there any job offers I declined or friendships I failed to pursue that would have put me on a radically different path? Would I have found more fulfillment trudging through the snow in Denver than experiencing the joys and pains of a New York City life? I know only too well that some seemingly small incident or the chance encounter with one individual can initiate a chain of events that lead to unimaginable consequences. But then, in the midst of my bucolic Rocky Mountain musings, I am assured by the knowledge that my life has indeed turned out very well. I realize that the people I hold so dear in this world would not be with me in any alternate existence and I soon find myself settling right back into my actual reality.

Reflections on what ifs and deliberations about chains of events always surfaced in my line of work. How many times did I avoid a devastating injury by being in the right place at the right time, by turning to the right rather than the left, or simply by not moving at all? There were a number of instances when I knew that I had been very fortunate and undoubtedly many other times when I was naïvely unaware of just how lucky I had been. And, always, the slightest change in just one element could have radically influenced that luck and altered the outcome.

Every fire was like that: a series of circumstances would start it, a string of factors would influence its growth, and a sequence of decisions spelled out just how devastating it would become. If I analyzed just about any fire I would often find that it could have been avoided altogether or at least would have been less destructive if at any point there was a break in the chain of events that had shaped it. But it was always the most damaging fire that made me think about how things could have been different. The incidents that caused massive destruction or staggering loss of life left me stunned and haunted by the devastation. I witnessed such an event when I was working as a lieutenant in the Bronx.

I had actually driven right past the scene two days before it all happened. It was a Thursday morning and, as always, I left home very early so I could allow the officer I was relieving plenty of time to pack up his gear and head home. So I was right on schedule and in no particular rush when I stopped for a traffic light on Southern Boulevard. And as I waited for the light to change I just happened to glance over and noticed a building to my right.

There were often times when I looked at buildings from a professional perspective. I might consider how it was constructed, observe where the means of egress were located, and note what kind of occupancy was inside the structure. It was kind of a mental exercise to sharpen my size-up abilities as a fire officer. It also had the added practical benefit of making me feel better prepared. You never knew which building would have a fire in the middle of the night. That was when you were under stress and it was cold and dark and difficult to see. If you had a chance to view it in the daytime before it ever burned you felt ahead of the game and were in a better position to conduct a safe operation.

But that was not my mindset as I sat in my car and gazed at this particular building. I had never even noticed the place before and was just kind of daydreaming when the sign on front caught my eye. It was a white, rectangular billboard that stood out from the red brick wall it was mounted on. The large black lettering indicated that this was the Happy Land Social Club. There was a small yellow smiley face emblem placed between the words "Happy" and "Lands" and it advertised that the hall was available for hire for "All Social Events." I couldn't quite put my finger on it but there was something very sad about the place. Perhaps it was my recently acquired upper middle-class suburban values kicking in but as I looked at it, I felt that it would be the last place I would ever want to use for any kind of gathering. Neither the building nor the surrounding streets were very appealing and for a split second I felt bad for those who, unlike myself, had not been blessed with better alternatives in their lives.

All of this passed through my mind in the few seconds I had to wait for the light to change. Then I immediately forgot about it and drove on to the firehouse to work an uneventful and forgettable day tour. Of course I had no way of knowing that in about 48 hours I would be returning to that building for one of the deadliest fires in the history of New York City.

I never actually saw the fire, only the aftermath. On Saturday I was working a tour in a different area of the Bronx. When I received the alarm in the middle of the night I was informed that there had been a fire in a night club with a number of fatalities. We were assigned to relieve a unit at the scene and, with the fire already extinguished, that meant we would have but one task—gathering the dead and placing them in body bags. I advised my men of our assignment and several of them stared at me in disbelief.

I had been to hundreds of nighttime fire scenes in the past and they all had a similar milieu. The flashing emergency lights were more intense and mesmerizing in the darkness. They seemed to almost compete with each other as they blinked from the tops of fire trucks and frantically heralded yet another misfortune. A reporter or two would usually be standing in the wings hoping to gather information for a few lines in a newspaper or for a minute of airtime before moving on to their next story. There was a sense of being on the cutting edge, of seeing and participating in an incident while the rest of the city slept. It was at nighttime, immediately after a fire, when you could still smell the smoke in the street and had to step cautiously around the charred debris that laid on the sidewalks. And though you were wide awake it was still hours away from daybreak when people would slowly approach and sadly comment on their neighbors' burned-out apartment or shocked employees would show up for work and stare at the charred remains of their place of business.

On this night the streets were congested with dozens of emergency vehicles and we had to park the rig several blocks from Happy Land. When I got near the building I could see that hordes of reporters had already lined the scene, all straining for a better view and hoping for more precise information about the disaster. It was clear that this place was different, that something monumental had occurred. I reported to the chief and he ordered me to take my company up to the second floor. We entered the building and took in a scene that is still etched in my mind.

There are times when you don't have anything in your mental repertoire to define or explain what you are seeing and your reaction to that sight is to deny its reality. And that was my exact reaction when we walked up a narrow stairway to reach the second floor of the club. There, lying right in front of us, were dozens of bodies. They all appeared to be very young and were sprawled throughout the entire floor. The strangest thing, aside from the overwhelming number of corpses, was the almost total absence of physical trauma. Except for the dark soot on the victims' nostrils there was very little apparent damage that could account for so many rapid deaths. It looked as though the hectic social gathering spot had been instantly transformed into a quiet rest area and they had all just suddenly decided to lie down and sleep. The silence of the room added to the improbability of the scene and I found myself groping with the reality vs. fantasy debate that was raging in my subconscious. There was nothing in my collection of mental images that could readily match the scene other than photos of the 1978 Jonestown mass suicide.

Still, my men and I were professionals with a job to accomplish. For the next several hours that job involved picking up the victims, placing them in body bags, and attempting to preserve anything that could assist in identifying them. It was not always easy to sort through who may have owned what. How did you figure out which pocketbook belonged to which woman when there were clusters of bodies piled so near to each other?

For us the task of matching a personal item to its likely owner was much more than an effort at providing an identification for a body. I think it was more like trying to give some dignity to them, to match them with a possession that meant something to them when they were alive, to gather the wallets, the make-up, the combs, and the phone numbers, all the personal stuff that surrounded them and retained their essence even though they were gone. It wasn't logical but it seemed so essential to get it right for their sake.

After a while I found myself focusing on one victim in particular. She was a very young woman who was still lying in the spot where she had lived the last few seconds of her life. Her dress was askew and the rest of her clothing was in a state of disarray that would have embarrassed her in life but in death gave evidence of how quickly she must have fallen. I looked at her and thought of how much care she must have taken in getting ready for this evening, the dress she thoughtfully selected, the hair she so stylishly groomed, and the phone calls she may have made to friends in anticipation of an exciting night out. She was a small girl and one of my men refused any help when he picked her up and placed her into a body bag. I remember him saying, "She's not a big girl" and he treated her remains very gently, almost as if she were still alive. I found his actions both touching and infuriating at the same time. I was moved by the respect he showed but also angry that her life was suddenly blotted out for no reason, that she was no longer a young girl with a future, just a dead woman who had the misfortune of being in the wrong place at the wrong time. And, worst of all, I thought about her mother, father, and siblings who were perhaps just hours away from getting a devastating phone call that would forever alter their lives.

Sadly, there were a lot of phone calls made that night and despite the enormity of the tragedy it was all the end result of just one man's enraged act. He had shown up that evening and argued with a girlfriend who worked in the club. The bouncer ejected him around 3 a.m. but he returned a short time later with a container of gasoline. In the midst of his fury he splashed and ignited the gas near the entranceway and sealed the fate of most of the club patrons. A total of 87 people died in Happy Land. The girlfriend who was the target of his wrath survived.

When we had completed our work and were leaving the scene I was approached by one of the news reporters. She asked me what it was like in there and I lied and told her that my unit had not been involved. I guess I was physically and emotionally fatigued and just couldn't come up with words to portray what we had just seen. We had all experienced fireground deaths but this was an off-the-scale experience that would not be surpassed in our minds until those jetliners crashed into two downtown high-rise buildings 11 years later.

There are a lot of odd circumstances in life. Happy Land occurred 79 years *to the day* from the 1911 Triangle Shirtwaist Fire where 146 people died. And I made my observations of the club just hours prior to the fire. Do I think that I "foresaw" something as I drove past it on that Thursday morning? No, I am far too much of a pragmatist to be lured into such mystical thinking. I'm sure that I must have stared at other buildings and glanced at a lot of other scenes as I drove into work that day. We are all bombarded with hundreds of images every day and I just happened to stumble upon one that turned out to be very significant.

Rather than thinking that I had any kind of prescient experience I am again drawn into thoughts about the eternal what ifs

The Happy Land Social Club fire, a disaster of historical consequences that took the lives of 87 people (photograph by Steve Spak).

of life. What if Julio Gonzalez had not given in to the demons that drove him that night and instead of setting the fire he had just stayed home alone and yelled and punched the wall to pacify the anger he felt toward his girl-friend? What if he had been unable to find a container to hold the $1 worth of gasoline he purchased at a nearby gas station? Or, for that matter, what if he had decided not to come to the United States from Cuba in the 1980 Mariel boatlift? Just one modification to any part of this chain of events and Happy Land would never have happened and 40 parents would not have lost children and about 90 children would not have become orphans. And that young woman we gently placed into a body bag almost 30 years ago might be here right now speaking to her own children. And she could tell them about a time when she was young and liked to put on a nice dress and dance to music in a night club.

A Discourse on Dirt

It is common knowledge that firefighting is a very dangerous job. At the same time it is also one of the dirtier career paths to follow. But we're not talking about dirt as in the topsoil you recently put in your flower bed or the stuff that was in the vacuum cleaner bag you just threw out. This is an entirely different species of dirt. Soot, smoke, and a plethora of carcinogens are an integral part of any fire, whether it's a $5 million condo or a cheap, pay-by-the-hour motel room that's burning. And, aside from the fire toxins, you cannot imagine some of the stuff that people will leave lying around in these places. I've had to deal with piles of moldering newspapers dating back to the Ford presidency, plastic trays of food left out for days, snakes or other exotic pets left to wander on their own, and the vomit of a dead junkie. To that must be added the animal and human feces encountered in the vacant building fires that still occasionally haunt sections of New York City. If you want excitement become a firefighter. But come wearing gloves.

However, grit and wear were not always interpreted as negatives in the fire service. Both the nature of the work and the job culture were at play in a firefighter's relationship with dirt. In fact, battered helmets and filthy turnout gear served as a red badge of courage. "Salty"-looking fire garb acted as a kind of Rosetta stone that provided a rapid interpretation of a firefighter's background. All of the dents, stains, and tears in your equipment were symbols that gave evidence of previous fire encounters and clearly delineated you from the inexperienced personnel and their immaculately clean gear.

The leather front piece of your helmet indicated which unit you were assigned to. If it was frayed and soiled to the point of illegibility you were granted a certain status on the fireground and assumed to have a high level of competence. Some firefighters would even bend down the rear sections of their helmets at a 90-degree angle to create the so-called "Brooklyn Bend" (or the "Bronx Bend" if you worked in the most poverty-stricken borough in New York City). Supposedly this provided better protection for your neck from hot water and falling embers but was really another expression of fireground machismo. I even worked with a probie who had had been on the job for just a few months and decided to put his shiny new helmet inside the kitchen oven to give it a more weathered appearance.

So grunge conferred status and, as with any group of people, status was important. But in today's FDNY worn-down fire gear is not always an accurate indicator of the depth of a man's firefighting resume. The job now has a quartermaster system in place that issues new gear and repairs items at no cost to the firefighters. Originally, new recruits entering the department had to lay out a substantial amount of money to purchase their equipment and any necessary repairs or replacements were done at their own expense. Joining the department meant laying out a capital investment of hundreds of dollars to start a new career.

To help defray those costs an annual uniform allowance was issued, appropriately enough, around Christmastime. Very often that money had already been spent on a child's gift or to help pay off a mortgage or some other household expense. If your boots were getting a bit worn or if your turnout coat had seen better days, expensive replacement items were not always at the top of the list in your budget priorities. You would more likely spend a few bucks at one of the shoe repair stores that mended fire gear as a sideline and fix an old item rather than replace it with a new one. As a result it was not uncommon to see turnout coats covered with leather patches and shoes worn in the firehouse that looked like they could have come off of a homeless bum. I personally went through three ranks and about 15 years on the job with my original firefighting turnout coat. That coat still hangs in a corner of my garage, patched and scared by the hundreds of fires I wore it to. It's going to be a difficult decision when the garage is finally cleaned out. Do I keep the coat or throw it out? Logic (and my wife) would tell me to just get rid of it. But that would feel like throwing out an important part of my past and must we always follow the logical choice?

Eventually I was issued a spanking new "bunker" ensemble that was not only clean but also afforded better protection from heat and flames. One of my prime theories about dirt was reinforced when I first wore my pristine new gear at a few fires. And that basic hypothesis is that the dirtier you get the less you care about being dirty. I noticed things when I wore the brand-new garb that I had never perceived before, like the greasy stains on my fresh coat after a fire in the oil burner room of an apartment building or the slick food waste clinging to my new polished boots after a job in the kitchen of a Chinese restaurant. For a while it was actually a bit disturbing to see the new gear getting soiled, something I had never felt with my previous clothing. My old gear had been so embedded with such a variety of filth that I didn't even notice when new indignities were added. It's kind of like shoveling a pile of cow manure (which I admittedly have yet to experience in my life). It would be distasteful at first but by the time you got down to the last few shovelfuls you would hardly take notice of your level of cleanliness.

But by far the most striking example of imperviousness to dirt I have witnessed occurred at the World Trade Center site. While working there one afternoon I saw some firefighters smelling pieces of debris to check for the scent of dead flesh. Months of exposure to dust and cadaver remnants had entirely desensitized them. Dirt is like disease. You adapt to it because it won't adapt to you.

I was a "covering" lieutenant while I was still wearing my old fire gear. That meant that I had no regularly assigned firehouse and was sent to work in any fire station in the city that needed an officer. It also meant traveling to and from work with my gear in the trunk of my car. After a fire my stuff was wet and reeked of smoke and I'd throw it into a plastic garbage bag. When I got home I hung it up in my basement until it dried and was ready for my next tour. Very often both the car and the basement smelled just like work.

On one occasion I had to remove a burned woman from an apartment fire. Though we don't often think of it as such, our skin is actually the largest organ in our bodies. And this unfortunate lady was covered with second degree burns. When that happens the skin easily peels off in sheets of dead tissue. I've even seen burned skin slide off of a victim's hands just like a glove. There is no way you can carry someone out of the chaos and stress of a fire without getting some contamination on your gear. However, it wasn't until I got home that I noticed there was still some of her skin clinging to my turnout coat. I immediately dropped the gear on my porch and used a mixture of water and bleach to clean it as best as I could. Today I'm sure that OSHA and a slew of other multi-lettered government agencies would have a fit over such a procedure. Back then you just kind of acclimated to it as another aspect of what was essentially a dirty line of work.

The era of salty firefighting gear and questionable cleaning procedures is now over. And good riddance to it. In this progressive era the FDNY requires periodic cleaning of a firefighter's gear to remove the built-up dirt and carcinogens. They also issue clean back-up equipment when necessary as well as a large duffle bag for transporting the gear to different work locations. That firefighter you may see humping a smoke-scented red bag through the streets probably has some dirty stuff inside but you can be sure he won't be taking it home.

Still, to me there is a strange dichotomy between the new era of cleanliness and the inherently sullied nature of the job. I have in my basement three helmets that I used over the course of my career. I wore the last one for only a short period. It sits there, bright, shining, and uncorrupted just like a museum piece. But while it may be great to look at, it just doesn't reflect my memories of the work. It is the other two old, beaten up, leather helmets still bearing the soot and the scars that mirror the physical reality of the work I did.

And perhaps in a very subtle way that physical reality was one of the appeals of the job. Much of our world today is sanitized. We are four hundred million years removed from the creature that first tentatively flopped from the ocean onto the land. Over that period we have created art, poetry, and the Kardashians. But at the same time we have become divorced from aspects of our physical existence. Is it possible that the growing separation from the corporeal world and a growing immersion in the ethereal domain has taken a toll on our emotional well-being?

Even in a digitalized world there are still sanitation workers, mechanics, and painters. But for many, if not most, people, workplace dirt now refers to stains on the collars or underarms of tailored dress shirts. Sawdust, oil, and grass stains are the realm of a growing minority who labor in jobs

I wore this helmet for most of my years as a chief. The dents and stains reflect the physical reality of the job (photograph by the author).

that deal with tangible objects. I understand the relevance of a 401(k), an IPO, and cloud computing. But what do these things look like, what color are they and how do they feel or smell? In contrast, the gritty but tangible aspect of my work was easy to grasp and experience. There was definitely a cerebral aspect in the art of firefighting. But the work also reaffirmed my role as a functioning person in a physical world, a world that involved smoke, water, dirt and other sensations you could taste and feel.

Perhaps Rene Descartes would have been just as astute had he written, "I sweat therefore I am."

A Brush with Mortality

After bouncing around the city for three years as a "covering" lieutenant I finally found a home base and was permanently assigned to a Bronx ladder company. This gave me an opportunity to get to really know the firefighters assigned to the unit as well as the neighborhood we responded to. It felt good to have some permanence in my work life. Knowing where and when I was scheduled to be on duty made it a lot easier to organize my busy life outside the job. And the job of supervising also got easier as I got to know the personalities and capabilities of my coworkers. I now knew which firefighters could be relied on for an especially vital assignment at a fire and which ones would step up for a dirty job in the firehouse. The moment I got to work I could instantly tell which guys would make me laugh and be a joy to work with and which ones might be a drag and require a bit closer supervision. I also learned about the intricacies of the "bad" buildings in our response area. Those were the buildings that could present firefighting nightmares because of renovations, previous fires, troublesome tenants, or other urban woes.

As it does in any profession one enjoys doing, time just flew by. Three years after being assigned to the company it was time to make another move. I got promoted to the rank of captain and once again started covering throughout the city. I couldn't have known it at the time but I was on a path that would eventually lead to one of the most frightening moments in my life.

For several weeks I was assigned to an engine company in Harlem. Back then it was not the up-and-coming, million-dollar brownstone area it has evolved into today. The Harlem of the early 1990s was still rather poor and plagued by drugs, vacant buildings, crime, and fires. In short, a great place for a firefighter to catch some good work. The area actually had a rich history. Starting in the early 20th century it had attracted a large black community that moved from the South for jobs and better lives in New York City. Harlem developed its own arts and music culture that was personified in famous night clubs like the Apollo, the Savoy Ballroom, and the Cotton Club where Duke Ellington and Cab Callaway launched their careers. Given the social prejudice that prevailed when it first opened in 1923 the Cotton Club was initially a "whites-only" night spot. By the time I showed up as a captain it seemed like the only Caucasians you regularly saw in the neighborhood were cops and firefighters. Just as in the Bronx there was often a wide social gap between the people who lived in poorer areas and the people who worked there keeping them safe.

My first few tours in the company were kind of uneventful with a number of responses for false alarms, routine emergencies and relatively minor fires. However, I had been around long enough to know how unpredictable the job was. You never wanted to allow yourself to get lulled into a sense of security or become lethargic. It seemed like just when you least expected it something very challenging and dangerous was just waiting to smack you in the head. The more time I spent on the job the more I understood and respected how dangerous the work could be. It was like the initial adolescent excitement of fighting a fire was gradually replaced by a more subdued middle-aged acceptance of the work, especially if you became an officer and were responsible for others.

As expected, the smack to my head came in the middle of a nice sunny day tour. We received an alarm for a fire on West 133rd Street. The building was a vacant, five-story brick tenement that had seen its heyday back when Cab Calloway was still belting out his "Hi-dee Hi-dee Hi-dee Hi's." It had since been reduced to a shell of a structure with empty rooms that sat, ghost-like, leaving no evidence of the many lives that had occupied them over the decades. The building still had a body but its soul was long gone. And when we arrived on the scene that body was burning fiercely.

As the first engine company our job was to connect to a hydrant, establish a reliable water supply, and position a hose line to confine and extinguish the fire. Or so the textbook said. The first part of that assignment went smoothly. The engine chauffeur hooked up to the nearest hydrant, my guys flaked out lengths of hose, and I led them into the first floor to start the attack on the fire. What I saw in there was actually kind of impressive.

I had been to a lot of tenement fires and they eventually became somewhat repetitive. At most of them I couldn't see very much initially, just a haze of smoke in the public hallway followed by a blast of hot blackness when the door to the fire apartment was forced open. Once I entered the apartment I would keep one of my gloved hands on a wall for guidance and then crawl forward through the darkness to search for the location of the fire. That was often the most difficult and nerve-racking task especially when I knew I was getting deeper and deeper into the maze of rooms and could sense that the intensity of the heat was rising. Eventually I would spot a bright glow emanating from the room that was burning. And once the nozzle was opened up and water was flowing the flames and dark smoke were instantly transformed into a cloud of steamy whiteness that would engulf me and reassure me that, once again, I had survived and conquered yet another fire.

However, the thing I witnessed as I looked up the stairway in this old Harlem building was an entirely different animal. All I could see was floor upon floor of fire. The building had sat vacant for a very long time and most of the windows and interior doors were missing. In effect it had been converted into a wide-open flue ideally designed to encourage the rapid spread of fire. This was no dark tenement job where I would have to grope through a smoky blackness just to locate the fire. Here there was almost no smoke at all, just a Hollywood-like display of a burning building complete with the added props of embers and chunks of flaming material floating down upon us from the upper floors.

Actually, I don't think that Hollywood has ever produced an accurate portrayal of what it's like to be in a fire. It's probably an impossible task since, in most fires, you are seldom able to see anything at all and that would make for some very uninteresting viewing. In most cases the fires that Ron Howard showed in *Backdraft* simply don't exist. But the inferno I saw as I looked up the stairs in this tenement appeared to be just like some of the scenes from the movie. And given that remarkable trait that allows the human mind to rapidly entertain multiple snippets of thought in any situation regardless of the distractions, I actually had a brief image of the film. It was as if Opie himself was comfortably seated in his director's chair on one of the upper floors calmly orchestrating the fire's intensity, changing the camera angles, and timing the release of flaming debris on the firefighters below.

We must have been inside the building for just a few seconds when that inner voice that guided me through so many fires started screaming, "This is a fire you are *not* going to conquer." And just as I was processing that thought the battalion chief arrived at the scene, sized up the situation, and came to the exact same conclusion. He got on the fireground radio and ordered everyone out of the building. The decision was made to give up the fight to save the structure because of the volume of fire, the relative worthlessness of the building, and the probability of nobody living there (although there was always the possibility of squatters living in an abandoned building—a thought that no doubt the chief considered in his decision). My men and I were closest to the rear exit of the first floor and we immediately started working our way toward the door.

We were still inside when it began. There are those moments in life when you know you are on the very edge of something horrible, that you have reached a tipping point that *will* lead to a disaster and there is no turning back. That moment when your car hits the patch of ice and you can see the tree you are about to smash into. That instant when you have lost your balance at the top of the ladder you've been using to paint the ceiling and you can feel yourself starting to fall. I had already spent many years in a career that put me in intimate contact with such events. Over and over I had seen the damage that followed those moments when all the negative factors meshed in perfect harmony to create a disaster. But those events had happened to *other* people, not to me, and I had been there to help out, to pick up the shattered pieces of other lives, not of mine.

I could hear it happening before any of my other senses were suddenly alarmed. We were still working our way to the rear exit when I heard a deep, overwhelming rumble that started high above us and grew in volume and intensity as it worked its way down to the first floor. The old tortured building had finally had enough. After decades of neglect and bombardment by the elements it had reached its tipping point and was starting to collapse. And unlike the many disasters I had witnessed as a firefighter, this was not happening to someone else, it was about to happen to me. Worse yet, it was also going to happen to the men I worked with. And in that deeply disturbing instant when I heard the rumble of falling bricks I felt that I had failed the people I was responsible for and had failed myself.

The darkness came just seconds after the sound. One moment I could clearly see my way to the exit and then, in a mere heartbeat, I was immersed in a cloud of utter blackness that didn't allow me to see anything at all. Despite the fact that it was bright and sunny outside the massive load of falling timbers and masonry pushed forward a cloud of dirt and soot that instantly obliterated any sense of daylight. And behind it all the sound of the tumbling bricks increased to a terrifying roar.

I never cease to wonder about the flexibility of the human mind. I was extremely scared, yet even in my fear I had a brief absurd thought when I heard the overpowering noise of the building collapsing around us. I had never been much of a literary critic but I didn't like when a writer described a noise as sounding like a freight train rolling down the tracks. It seemed so trite, like the author wasn't creative enough or just got lazy. Yet, in the middle of all that was happening, I noted that that was *precisely* what this sounded like. Here I was, on the verge of meeting Jesus, or Allah, or Odin, or eternal nothingness and for a brief instant all I could think was "Damned if some things actually *do* sound like a freight train."

Such a thought remained in my head for only a millisecond as I stood in that dark cloud on the first floor. It was instantly replaced by the terror that reached deep into my core. But at the same time I felt a real sense of *sadness*, an immense regret that this life I loved so much, and all the people in it, was about to be obliterated. And I had only myself to blame. It was my choice of a career and my effort at being promoted that had placed me in this situation.

I knew that I wasn't alone. Before the choking blackness engulfed us I saw two of my men moving toward the rear exit. Another firefighter had been standing somewhere just to my left and I blindly reached out to locate him. I found him instantly and wrapped my arm around him and he did the same thing to me and we moved together, arm in arm, toward the exit. That was the most frightening time. He had my back and I had his but for a few seconds neither of us knew if we would make it out in time. In a strange way an abrupt end would have been easier to deal with than those torturous few moments when we waited for an unimaginable crushing impact and wondered if we had enough time to escape.

Funny thing about humans. They are often at their best when things are at their worst. That firefighter had reached out for me in the exact same way I had reached for him. Despite the fear he too must have felt he was not going to just run out and abandon his officer. And I was not going to leave without him.

All of these thoughts were put on hold once I was outside. Standing there in the rear of the building, back in the sunlight, back in life, I did all the things an officer was supposed to do. I accounted for the presence of all of my men, made sure we were a safe distance from the collapse zone, and reported to the battalion chief with my radio. I think that I clung to my role of captain because it was my job but at the same time I hadn't quite accepted the reality of what had just happened. A major portion of the old tenement had totally collapsed. The metal door jamb we had just passed through on our way out was completely bent out of shape by the falling debris. And I wasn't sure just what to feel. Relief? Elation? It was more like a simple numbness.

When I look back I can't seem to fully appreciate how lucky I was to survive this experience just as I tend take for granted the exceptionally good fortune I have had in so many other situations in life. It seems as though the accidents and injuries that do hurt us leave more of an impression than the bad things that don't happen to us. Perhaps it is denial or just a manifestation of "not me" syndrome, that belief that disaster and pain and even death are just concepts and not reality, things we are personally immune to and that only apply to others.

However, I did walk away from that building with two lessons vividly reinforced. The first was about the "Brotherhood," an expression that is so often used in the fire service that it sometimes loses its significance.

For all of the exhaustion, sleep deprivation, occasional bureaucratic an-noyances, and missed holidays with your family, in this line of work you did make a rather unique connection with your coworkers. If you crawled into a burning building with another firefighter, or ran out of a collapsing one, you shared an experience that created an unspoken bond, a kind of intimacy that can't really be duplicated in most professions or even fully explained to friends or family members outside of the firefighting world. As a "covering" officer I wasn't in a position to really know much about that guy I ran out of the building with. But regardless of the danger, and despite our fear, we had our arms protectively wrapped around each other as I looked out for him and he looked out for me.

The other lesson was about decisiveness and how one timely decision made by one individual can affect so many in an inherently dangerous job. A major section of that building collapsed and there was not a single injury. However, it would be inaccurate to label the incident as any sort of "miracle." That would imply that it was fate alone that determined the out-come. On the contrary, it was all the result of an order given by one man, the guy in charge, the battalion chief who was standing out in the street, supervising, evaluating, and weighing alternatives. It was he alone who made the right call in that delicate balance that exists between knowing when you have given it enough of a shot and when it's time to call it quits. In short, just doing his job as a chief and being able to "pull the trigger," change the entire strategy of the fire fight, and withdraw all of us from the building. You won't see his name in any newspaper article. He received no medal or commendation for his actions. But his gut reaction to pull us out undoubtedly spared a number of firefighters from dying on that sunny day in a sad old Harlem building.

This would be etched deep in my memory when I eventually became a chief and would also experience that lonely, uncomfortable position of making quick, difficult fireground decisions that could determine the sur-vival of others.

Lost in Translation

Like any large organization the FDNY made ample use of detailed procedures, catchy acronyms, and esoteric terminology. They were useful on the fireground, a place where quick and effective communication was so vitally important. Our firefighters used those procedures to coordinate their tasks at a fire and, regardless of what section of the city they were assigned to, they generally worked very well together. That was not always the case when we operated with other government agencies. Each agency had its own procedures, priorities, and bureaucratic jargon and their methods did not always mesh with our way of doing things. Sometimes there were even differences between the terms used by various fire departments. In New York City, for example, a "rescue" company was a unit that had expertise in building collapse scenarios, high angle rope operations, and other specialized activities. In other cities a "rescue" was an ambulance. Then there was the "rescue" work performed by the urban search and rescue units that existed in every state. The definition of what a rescue unit actually was depended on where you came from.

There was always a lot of room for confusion on the fireground. Communication problems and compatibility issues most often surfaced when several different city agencies were involved at the same incident. When bureaucracy met bureaucracy I sometimes found myself fighting semantics as well as the fire. There were times when I longed for the simplicity of a good, basic, FDNY fire operation where we all spoke the same language.

Following 9/11 efforts were made to help different government agencies work more effectively with each other. Homeland Security Presidential Directive-5 (HSPD-5) was established by the White House in 2003 in an attempt to unify and coordinate the work of multiple organizations at an emergency. It fostered the use of common terminology and the incident command system (ICS) as disaster management tools. It definitely took some getting used to. The FDNY had been using a version of ICS since its inception but the new language it required felt alien to someone like myself who had been on the job for a long time. ICS was well intended and could occasionally be useful but it could also become rather intricate. I experienced fires that got needlessly complicated when the chiefs felt a need to fill all of the command structure positions that existed in ICS. We could now call for the "Water Resource Officer" to establish a water supply rather than yelling, "Engine 3, get the fucking hydrant *now*!" An operation would still have an "Incident Commander" but there were times when he might be functioning with someone else in a "Unified Command," whatever the heck that meant. In addition, there might also be an "Operations Chief" and multiple "Division" officers. As we struggled to adapt to the new structure there were times when company officers weren't entirely sure of exactly who they had to report to.

If you liked abbreviations the new speak of modern incident command was ready for you. Thumbing through a booklet of terminology that was issued by FEMA, I discovered that ACAMS was an "automatic continuous air monitoring system," ACP meant "access control point," and a SOFA was not something to sit on but a "status of forces agreement." Some contractions even had several meanings. PD could stand for "per diem," "police department," "policy directive," or "presidential declaration." Certainly, learning Mandarin could be no more difficult than mastering this new language. But perhaps the most impressive expression of bureaucratic eloquence I uncovered was in a memo issued by the NYC Urban Area Working Group (UAWG) which informed us that the Regional Emergency Liaison Team (RELT) had been used successfully to share information with UAWG jurisdictions regarding H1N1 issues. I haven't quite yet figured out that one.

Two general schools of thought evolved when new ICS terms and concepts were introduced to the FDNY. The majority were at least indifferent to it all or, in some cases, outright reluctant to adapt to the changes. These were usually people, like myself, who had been fighting fires for a long time using the "street smart" language and long standing procedures that had always worked for us in the past. The thinking was "We fight a lot of fires, ICS is for small departments out in Iowa, not for us." On the other hand, there were some who ate up the new changes. That clique tended to thrive on bureaucracy and had a craving for systems that were resplendent with multi-lettered, military-like acronyms. The more management-sounding stuff they had to use the better they liked it.

Added to all of this were the intricately detailed systems that were already in place in the procedural manuals of the FDNY and other city agencies. Those systems *usually* worked but, because they were somewhat complex, at times they too were awkward to actually put into use. They also provided a vast amount of additional study material for me to master when I took a promotional exam. Included in that material was a dense 45-page bulletin on emergency command procedures. That particular volume was a bureaucratic work of art which used terms like "public personnel carrier" rather than referring to something as a "bus." When I plowed my way through a marathon reading of the bulletin its use of verbiage like public personnel carriers really turned me off. I mean, why can't we just call a thing what it is? A bus is a bus, for goodness sake. Ralph Kramden drove the damn thing on *The Honeymooners.*

My big question regarding any procedure was did it actually work when the shit was hitting the fan or could the very complexity of a system strangle its effectiveness just when we most needed it? One day working a tour as a captain in the South Bronx I kind of got my answer. I was in a ladder company and we were first due for a smoke condition in a subway tunnel that ran under the Harlem River between the Bronx and Manhattan. The policy called for us to request a "light" train to transport firefighters into the tunnel to investigate the cause of the smoke. A light train was a subway that had a transit authority motorman and a conductor but no passengers on board. Since fireground radios did not allow us to communicate from the tunnel up to the street the plan also called for the train motorman to establish a workable radio link for us. My job was to inform the motorman of the message I wanted relayed to the fire department. He in turn was to relay that information to the transit authority dispatcher through his radio link which was capable of functioning from inside the tunnel. The transit dispatcher would forward my message to the fire department dispatcher who would then communicate with fire units that were standing by up in the street. A bit complex but workable. I had used the relay system successfully in the past but on this day I would learn that any procedure, just like any chain, was only as strong as its weakest link.

I boarded the train with two of my men and just before leaving the station I informed the chief who was located up in the street that we were about to enter the subway tunnel to investigate a smoke condition. We must have been some 200 yards into the tunnel when the train stopped and the motorman opened one of the car doors. Even though I had experienced this numerous times before it still felt strange to be stepping out into the dark recesses of the tunnel rather than the familiar confines of a station. We got onto to the narrow, grimy catwalk that ran next to the track and began our long, cautious walk deeper into the tunnel.

Like most New Yorkers I had ridden subway trains for much of my life but that background had been limited to experiencing just the inner world of the subway car. I had mastered the urban skill of gracefully scooting into an unimaginably crowded car without stepping on someone. I learned to avoid eye contact with fellow passengers even as I shared closer physical intimacy with them than I did with some of my girlfriends. And I developed the ability to maintain a grip on any pole or handle that would keep me and four or five other people from falling when the train suddenly bucked. The outside world of the subway tunnel was a dark, uninviting realm that nobody ever visited. It was a space of mesmerizing blackness that raced by the car windows as the train sped through, punctuated by the occasional dingy yellow light bulb and an endless array of vertical, dust covered I-beams.

I had to occasionally do my work in that hidden world when I became a firefighter. Although I learned how to survive and function safely in the subway catacombs I never fully overcame my basic discomfort with being there. And with good reason. Subway tunnels were very dangerous places. The catwalks we walked on were narrow, the place was dusty and dimly lit, and, even if the power had been reported to be turned off, we had to maintain a constant awareness of the third rail which carried a fatal electric charge. On top of it all there were "no clearance" areas which were to be avoided at all costs because they did not allow enough room to stand between the tunnel wall and the side of a passing train. I didn't even want to imagine what kind of death I would experience if I was suddenly caught there when an unexpected train sprang out of the darkness.

My men and I were fully aware of these dangers as we prepared to leave the security of our train car. I followed the established procedure and approached the motorman to set up lines of communication before we stepped out on the catwalk. He was a middle-aged guy with the glazed, myopic look of a man who had spent many years roaring through tunnels and peering through the shadows of his subterranean world.

"Are you in touch with the transit dispatcher?" I inquired.

"What for?" he responded.

"To set up the relay between the transit and fire dispatchers," I explained, which immediately elicited another perplexed "What?" from him.

I couldn't figure out if the motorman was being hostile or was just confused. Probably there were elements of both. He was accustomed to maintaining established schedules and driving trains that were full of passengers. Stopping an empty train with three firefighters on it in the middle of a tunnel was beyond the scope of his daily routine.

I mentioned the "fire/transit communication protocol" that had been created for this exact scenario. Now he seemed really annoyed and asked, "What the fuck is that?"

I started to say that he would speak to his dispatcher and his dispatcher would speak to my dispatcher and my dispatcher would then speak to my chief up on the street and that's how it would all work, but even as I was telling him this I knew that it was all gibberish to him. On some level I guess I had my own suspicions about how much I could rely on the long string of messages. At the very least there would be delays in relaying any information. Ultimately it would come down to relying on myself and my two firefighters. We had our air masks, and if we timed it properly, we could count on having at least 10 minutes to go further into the tunnel, figure out what was causing the smoke, and get back to the reassuring confines of the train.

Fortunately, the smoke was not that thick when we left the car and I knew that the electricity had been turned off on the third rail so, short of another subway coasting through without power, we were unlikely to encounter any more trains further ahead. Still, it seemed like an eerie place to be in. The air was cool and the tunnel was extremely quiet, a strange contrast to the ear-piercing sound of screeching metal and steady beat of thumping train wheels that I had always associated with the place. The only sounds came from the steady, mechanical noise of my men's breathing apparatus. It was as if I had two Darth Vaders following closely behind me and it was reassuring to know that I was not alone.

We continued to slowly plod forward on the catwalk, further and further into the tunnel, constantly aware of our distance from the train and the amount of air we had left in our masks. I was willing to make a solid effort to scope out the location and intensity of the fire but I was certainly not going to put us beyond a safe point.

In a few minutes we found it—a small pile of rubbish quietly burning away in the middle of the track, no doubt started by sparks from a previous passing train. It turned out to be "five cents" worth of fire that had no real danger of getting any bigger, but hidden in the confines of the long tunnel, it had created enough smoke to seriously disrupt the transit system. We quickly extinguished the fire and rode the train to the Manhattan side of the tunnel for our exit back up to the street.

I was confident throughout the operation that things would work out. There were two solid guys working with me and we were following a plan that had been used on numerous occasions. However, I would not have felt so reassured had I been aware of two other developments that unfolded while we were under the river. The motorman had (not surprisingly) failed to set up any semblance of my requested communications relay. In addition, up in the street my own battalion chief had for some reason not only gone back to the firehouse but had also ordered all of the other fire units to leave the scene. Way down, deep in a tunnel beneath a river, my men and I were about as alone as three guys could possibly be in a city that had millions of people living in it. To this day I'm not sure if my final radio message to the chief telling him we were boarding a light train was ignored or misunderstood. But I do know that a small team of firefighters was briefly placed into circumstances it should never have been in.

Fortunately, this turned out to be a minor incident. I got lucky as I did so many times in my career. Had it been a more intense fire, two firefighters, one captain, and one somewhat hostile train motorman could have been in some serious trouble. The system had failed to work as planned. No communications link had been established. A procedure that looked so good on paper just did not function. Such failures are often rectified by the actions of one individual. In this case my very experienced company chauffeur decided to drive the rig to the Manhattan side of the tunnel which he knew would be the nearest point to our exit from the subway. He also stayed in communication with the fire dispatcher who in turn immediately reassigned a (somewhat embarrassed) chief and all of the other units back to the scene. Needless to say, after this incident, that particular chief was not on the list of fire commanders I felt confident working with.

The experience reinforced a basic firefighting premise I strongly believed in: simpler is always better. There are times when concise, well-thought-out plans will not work, especially in the confusing and stressful domain of the fireground. A complex procedure that can look so workable on paper can just as easily fall apart and strangle itself when real people put it into effect. Ultimately the beauty of any system lies not in the details but in how well it works.

I concur with the Thoreau quote: "Our lives are frittered away with detail. Simplify, Simplify." But I prefer what Ralph Waldo Emerson wrote in response when he pointed out to Thoreau, "One 'Simplify' would have sufficed."

I think Ralph and I would have worked well together.

Letters in the Attic

I probably would never have become a firefighter if it wasn't for my father. I like to think that I would have been a good teacher or skilled carpenter or possibly even a police officer. But most likely I would have become a somewhat inept and disinterested administrator performing some unstimulating role in a corporate or government office. Prior to the FDNY I had attended college and bounced around aimlessly for a number of years. I had always worked at some job and generally enjoyed an active and sometimes frantic social life. I met a lot of women, experienced a couple of short-lived relationships, and overall had very little permanence in my life. But my work was never the source of my fulfillment or related to my interests. In short, I had a happy existence that had followed the normal go to college, go to work path. And that existence was extremely sheltered from the experiences that awaited me in the fire department.

Like so many other firefighters I "inherited" the job from a family member. Firefighting is not an occupation that most people think of when it's time to send out resumes. With a father in the FDNY I had been exposed to that world from an early age. But unlike a lot of firefighters' sons I never held a childhood dream of becoming a firefighter. I always kind of viewed it as a very different and exciting lifestyle rather than an occupation. I watched as they fought fires in my Brooklyn neighborhood and was impressed by how well they performed under pressure. It was like they were in combat rather than just doing a job. And there was something very appealing about the urgency of the fire trucks as they raced through the streets speeding toward that battle. These guys were different. It seemed like most of the people in the neighborhood plodded off to their factory or office jobs with a sense of boredom if not absolute dread. My dad and his friends couldn't wait to get to work.

So when my father urged me to fill out the application papers, I did. And then, for about two years, I kind of forgot about it. Like a lot of good things in my life, the job offer came along at just the right time. It wouldn't have come at all were it not for my dad.

But it wasn't like I didn't earn it. The New York City firefighter's exam was generally given every four years and was extremely competitive. Even in good economic times when there were variety of other career options available more than 20,000 applicants took the test. To have any shot at getting hired you had to score very well on both a written exam and a rigorous physical test followed by a comprehensive medical and background investigation.

I trained for the physical like I was preparing for the Golden Gloves. I would get up at 6 a.m. and run five miles before I went to my office job. On really cold mornings I got motivated by picturing scenes from *Rocky* (yes, out of curiosity I once did drink a glass of raw eggs, and no, I did not get salmonella. But I never dated a girl named Adrian). When I got home from work it was time for weightlifting. I still didn't really view the fire department as a lifetime career. It was more like the application process itself became a challenge. And I attacked that challenge with all the gusto I had.

That intensity carried over once I got on the job. Over the years I managed to get promoted four times. I wasn't brilliant but I did have an ability to dedicate an enormous amount of time to studying the massive volumes of firefighting tactics, laws, and administrative procedures that were covered in the promotional exams. The competition for the lieutenant, captain, battalion chief, and deputy chief tests was about as keen as the original marathon contest that was required to get on the job. One of my fellow firefighters had attended law school and he told me that he hadn't studied as hard for the bar exam. I had never put in as much effort when I was attending college. At times it seemed like being intelligent was a detriment in preparing for the tests since it was essentially a process that required rote memorization and the ability to recognize the correct answer on a multiple-choice exam. The FDNY wasn't looking to promote rocket scientists but determined firefighters who were willing to put in the time to prepare for supervisory jobs. And those were often more dangerous jobs that entailed a great deal of responsibility for the safety of men they would lead on the fireground.

Fortunately my hard work paid off and on four separate occasions my family and I got to attend promotional ceremonies. In truth, I had never really liked ceremonies. At one point in my past I had actually been an altar boy and endured seemingly endless religious rituals that were conducted in Latin. But I had long since rejected organized religion and found that just about any kind of ceremony turned me off whether it was religious, political, or old-timers' day at Yankee Stadium. Despite that, I enjoyed the FDNY promotional events because of the joy it gave my parents, particularly my father. I can still picture him excitedly writing down my designated battalion on a small piece of paper when our assignments were announced at my lieutenant promotion. It was as if he was flashing back several decades and was once again being promoted himself.

My father also got to attend the ceremony on the day I was promoted to captain. I know that one was especially significant for him. He was on the captain's promotion list himself when he had retired as a lieutenant almost 20 years prior and had often expressed regret that he did not stay on the job to achieve that rank. Looking back, he was 60 years old when he retired and another promotion would have required him to travel around the city and work in some very busy areas at a time when there was still a considerable amount of fire activity in the FDNY. It was probably better that he hadn't done that. Still, I understood his frustration and think that watching me receive the silver bars of a captain's insignia gave him some sense of completion.

That would be the last promotional ceremony he would see. Not long after he was diagnosed with Parkinson's disease. When I found out I knew that it was bad but didn't really know what to expect and I watched help-lessly as he began to physically deteriorate. In his prime he had been much physically stronger than I had ever been. As a child I marveled when he effortlessly dove deep into a lake to retrieve an object someone had acci-dentally dropped over the side of a boat. Even when he was on vacation, at his core he was still a fireman. One time I saw him dash instantly into the water to save a young boy from drown-ing. And at the age of 56 he had easily picked me up from the floor and carried me to a bed when I passed out because of an illness. I remember regain-ing my senses as he was carry-ing me and wondering how he could so easily maneuver my 170 pounds.

As time went on this sturdy man who had served others for

My father in the Army during World War II (Dunne family photograph).

decades as a soldier, police officer, and firefighter was no longer capable of caring for himself and he had to rely on help when performing tasks as simple as buttoning his shirt. Never once did I see him complain about his affliction. The mental confusion had to be even more difficult for him to endure. I'm not sure if he ever finished high school but he had been a passionate reader and could always hold an intelligent conversation on a variety of topics. The degenerative impact of the disease ended all that. Of all the effects of Parkinson's it is the swallowing up of a personality that is the most disturbing.

Eventually he had to stay in a nursing home. I went through the process of visiting and evaluating several, hoping to find one that would provide the appropriate care and atmosphere. Some were better than others but, by their very nature, they were all sad environments. Placing him in any of them was almost like sending your child off to sleep-away camp. I worried about how reliable the staff would be and how he would be treated. The home I chose seemed like the best alternative in a difficult choice with no pleasant alternatives.

I visited him in the home at least once a week. We would hang out in his room and on nice days I would take him outside to a small garden area just outside the building. It was actually kind of Zen-like and relaxing. He enjoyed the fresh air and I enjoyed his company along with the satisfaction of knowing I was adding just a little variety to his daily routine. On his good days we spoke a bit and I would tell him what was going on with my family and on the job. We were doing something that we had never actually done since I had become an adult—hanging out together, just the two of us. When it was time for me to leave I would tell him I'd see him next week and he would usually respond by saying "Don't bother," but not in an angry way. He just didn't want me to take the time from my busy life to come back. But, of course, next week would come and I would be anxious to see him again.

My father's good days did not last long. His ability to speak and at times to even recognize me became increasingly rare and difficult. Before I would go upstairs to see him I would often have to sit in my car for a minute to psych myself up for the supportive but painful visit. My sadness was only assuaged by the thought that he seemed not to be suffering as he drifted off into a state of confusion.

I got promoted to battalion chief about a year after he entered the nursing home and it was the first FDNY ceremony he could not attend. I wished so much for him to know that I had actually become a chief but at that point he was usually so far gone that he seldom comprehended what was going on around him. Only on rare occasions would there be a brief spark of recognition, like the time he saw my three-year-old son in his room.

One day I happened to be working in a battalion not far from the nursing home and I dropped by to see him. When I entered the lobby in my FDNY uniform one of the administrators started freaking out, thinking I was there for some kind of surprise inspection or audit of their records. Another woman who had often seen me immediately told her to relax—she knew I was just there to visit my father. I sat with him for a while in his room and he was in his usual oblivious condition. But at times he would stare at some object like he was in deep thought. Soon he was gazing intently at the battalion chief's insignia on the shoulder of my uniform jacket. And in that brief instant when his eyes quickly flashed from the insignia to my face, he knew.

I was on duty in a rundown Brooklyn neighborhood when my father died. When I got the phone call several firefighters I didn't even know immediately came up to my office to offer their help and condolences. As always, those tough, loud, blue-collar guys showed their dignity and their class. It was raining when I headed home, and as I drove through the gray Brooklyn streets, I was hit with a powerful sense of beginning a journey. I was starting that part of my life when my father was actually gone.

Sometime later I went back to the nursing home to gather his things. There was little in the room to indicate he had even been there. Just a small piece of furniture, a television, and a pile of his clothing. I took his clothes home with the intent of giving them away. And I just couldn't get myself to do it. Even though I knew it made no sense, it felt like giving up his garments was like giving away a part of him. I kept his goose down winter coat and to this day I wear it myself on really cold days. The rest of the stuff went up in the attic, where it remained undisturbed for a long time.

I had put a lot of work into fixing up the attic when I first moved into the house, installing insulation and putting down flooring. When I was cleaning out the debris that had been left up there by the previous owner I uncovered a decades-old auto repair bill. I threw the bill out but remember thinking about how long it had been hidden away in a corner of the attic. Long after my father died I went back up there to retrieve a suitcase. I saw his clothes and suddenly thought about the old repair bill I had found. It occurred to me that I had never gone through any of the pockets in my father's garments. Suddenly I got excited and wondered if there might possibly be something tucked away inside any of them. I guess I was hoping for a letter or a note or even a bus pass, anything that might illuminate a small part of his existence and provide some kind of connection, however tenuous.

I never did find anything in those pockets. But looking back I do know that for a brief moment in a sad little nursing home room, a message had indeed been exchanged between the two of us.

A Jane Doe

I don't know if she was still alive when I first saw her. She appeared to be a relatively young woman and was lying on her back on the gray sidewalk. Her light clothing suited the early morning summer weather but I remember thinking that she had to be uncomfortable feeling the cool, hard concrete against her body. Discomfort was the least of her struggles. Emergency medical personnel were moving around her limp body, aligning the tubes and oxygen source that fed a plastic face piece covering her mouth and nose. One of them was rhythmically moving up and down as he performed CPR in a desperate effort to bring her back to consciousness.

I started the long walk up to her apartment while EMS continued their work. The stairway was just like countless others found in the drab, worn-out tenements that defined the neighborhood. Seemingly endless marble steps wound their way up a dark, stifling interior that was occasionally punctuated by illegible spray-painted graffiti. Streams of water dripped down the stairway and I carefully stepped over the charged hose line that snaked around each turn. When I saw the soot-stained walls and smelt the pungent remnant of smoke I knew that I had arrived on the fire floor.

The apartment turned out to be a "Collyer's Mansion," a term derived from the name of two brothers who lived in Harlem years ago in a building that was filled floor to ceiling with worthless junk and debris. The woman had likewise collected mountains of odd possessions, much of which spilled out into the public hallway from her apartment door. The evidence of her private neurosis had become a public spectacle as firefighters sloughed through piles of old newspapers, rumpled clothing, and the detritus resulting from years of obsessive hoarding.

Fire is the great equalizer. All burned-out apartments end up looking and smelling the same whether they are exclusive Manhattan condos or tiny hovels in run-down neighborhoods. The same drenched mix of soaked papers, photos, and scorched mattresses scattered about gives no

Typical tenement stairs. How many thousands of steps did I take on these when I grew up in Brooklyn and then over the course of a firefighting career (photograph by the author).

sign of the importance such items may have held in the life of the fire victim. I began to search through the debris for some bill, letter, or other piece of mail that would provide the woman's identification. Speaking to the other tenants in the building had proven to be fruitless. It seemed that they all knew her by sight but nobody knew her name. Her anonymity sadly fit the lifestyle she had been living in her home.

As firefighters continued to overhaul and search the apartment I received word that the woman had died at a local hospital. I noted that the smoke detector on the ceiling did not work and couldn't help but wonder what her final moments had been like. Had she suffered through moments of panic as the biting smoke started to overwhelm her or had she just drifted off into unconsciousness, unaware of what was happening?

Anyone who works in a profession that regularly deals with death knows that the only real dividing line that exists among us has nothing to do with race, religion, or politics. Ultimately, the only significant separation is the one between those who are alive and those who are not.

I have seen a great deal of death in my career and for the most part handled it very well. In fact, I sometimes feel guilty at how little it has bothered me. Perhaps it's like dealing with a disease. Steady exposure to something makes you somewhat immune to it. I have found that the really burned or damaged bodies are easier to deal with. They have lost their sense of humanity and seem more like fire-damaged material rather than remnants of what had once been a human being.

The woman I had seen lying on the sidewalk looked very much like a living person. And now, having witnessed the intimate details of her cluttered home and sensed the aloneness of her life, I thought her abrupt end seemed like a sad punctuation to her existence. Outside the building the day's normal activities went on as the neighborhood and the city woke up, untouched by the loss of one more individual. Life went on, as it always does, and as it should.

I went home, fatigued, shortly after the fire. Another 24-hour tour had ended. But I found myself especially appreciative of the warm breeze and clear sky that promised another nice summer day. My profession reinforced the reality that dark, parallel worlds exist, that every peaceful, safe environment is often counterbalanced by a setting in which someone is suffering. But rather than upsetting me, that knowledge always made me more appreciative of the good things that are also present in life.

However, on this beautiful morning one more name was going to be entered into the national database of fire fatalities. Her death would be a mere ripple in the pond. The poor neighborhood she lived in would not draw out the media as other sections of the city did and her passing would earn just a brief mention in the local press. But later on, as I enjoyed the day, I couldn't help thinking about the woman that nobody knew.

Commanding Stress

I kept hoping to finally hear some good news. It had been well over an hour since I first arrived at the hospital and things were not going well. It seemed like so much was happening but I could gather very little information either from my own personnel or the hospital staff. It was a constant effort just to fight off the endless bombardment of distractions. Noise from the blaring fireground radios echoed off the tiled walls of the lobby and mixed with the nervous banter of the large crowd that stood nearby. It was hard for me to hear anything, much less concentrate on what I was doing. And it was hot. With the air-conditioning system shut down the atmosphere was getting more and more oppressive and my fire coat was feeling heavier and heavier. The litany of problems kept rolling in, all with a sense of urgency. Patients needed assistance, battalion chiefs needed to relieve their firefighters with fresh personnel, the upper echelons downtown wanted a detailed update on what was going on. I was a brand-new deputy chief, the guy in charge, the one who would ultimately be held responsible, and I was starting to feel overwhelmed.

A major electrical problem had knocked out power to a four-block area and created a smoke condition in a basement which had drifted its way up to the seventh floor. The heavy concrete construction of the building interfered with my radio transmissions to the firefighters upstairs and I could make out little of what they were trying to communicate to me. I desperately needed some clear information on what was happening so I ordered a company to walk up and attempt to establish a radio relay back to me in the lobby. Moments later the building engineer informed me that the hospital's emergency generators were malfunctioning and there was a possibility of complete power loss. If that happened the effects on patient care could be disastrous. A trickle of sweat rolled down my back as I contemplated my predicament in the 90-degree heat.

Firefighting is routinely listed in the top 10 on lists of the most stressful occupations in America. Anyone who has commanded a complex fire or emergency has experienced the mental and psychological pressures of that position, especially if the operation was going poorly. Multiple tasks, incomplete or conflicting information, and the high stakes involved in life-and-death decisions all contribute to making firefighting a uniquely challenging profession.

I had managed fires quite often when I was a battalion chief. As the first chief officer at the scene I was responsible for sizing up the situation, establishing a strategy, and supervising the tactics for the initial attack on the fire. However, I was always operating in a position of temporary responsibility. Within a short time the deputy chief would arrive and assume command of the fire. I would meet with the deputy in the street, let him know what I had done up to that point, and then, relieved of overall command, I would go inside the building to supervise an individual segment of the fire. If it was a really tough and complex incident there was a sense of relief when the deputy got there. He was now running the whole show and I could concentrate on a smaller part of that job. Although a battalion chief had a very important role, a deputy was really the guy who could set the course for a safe and successful operation. He was in a position to make decisions that would save lives. But he could also kill people if he messed up and made the wrong decision.

I knew exactly what I was getting into when I got promoted to the deputy rank. I was now going to be "the man," the guy who would have to evaluate everything that was happening and decide if an operation should continue to follow the same course of action or if a radical change in strategy was needed. Sometimes this meant making the tough choice to just give up the building and withdraw everyone back down to the street. These were hard decisions that had to be made quickly and often without very obvious clues. Not everything in firefighting was black and white; there were a lot of gray areas. When I was a deputy it would be a long time before a superior who I could turn to for advice would be on the scene. I would soon learn the meaning of "the loneliness of command." I was not only going to be fighting fires, I was also going to be fighting my own stress.

Every level of firefighting was stressful but the nature and intensity of that stress changed as I climbed the pecking order of rank in the department. When I was a firefighter I couldn't wait for my next fire and felt frustrated if I missed a tough job that came in on a day I was not working. Even though I was aware of the danger I felt relatively unstressed by the work. Part of that was due to adrenaline. It was exciting work and, while there was always a level of uncertainty in the chaos of the fireground, you were able to exert some physical control over your environment. You could open up the hose nozzle on fire that suddenly appeared or intensified. You could use a search rope to guide your way out of a building in thick smoke. You always carried some kind of tool in your hands and could use that tool to smash your way through a door or even a wall if you were in trouble. You were physically involved at a fire but you were generally responsible for no one but yourself. You worked as part of a team and each member watched out for the other. But you were not the leader of that team and, while you had to account for your actions, you would not be held responsible for the overall success of the incident. In a sense you got to do the fun, hands-on stuff while the company officer or chief generally took the blame if things went south.

Being a firefighter was certainly not easy or devoid of stress. But for me at least much of that stress derived from the erratic work hours and sleep deprivation or from the realities of being cooped up for 24 hours in the firehouse, sometimes with coworkers who were not easy to be with. One guy I worked with likened it to being in prison. We all wore the same clothing, ate communal meals, worked out with weights, occasionally bitched and moaned, and, always, tried to maintain our status in the alpha male atmosphere of the work environment.

The rank of lieutenant was my first step up the promotional ladder. As a company officer I was directly responsible for the well-being of the four or five people assigned to my unit and not just for my own safety. When I was the first officer to arrive at a job I was, at least for a few brief minutes, in a position to give orders and plan the initial attack on the fire. And for the first time I experienced the frustration of supervision. I could no longer physically perform the work myself. I had to rely on others to comply with my orders to get the work accomplished. That meant communicating my intentions effectively and learning to trust that my men would perform as I intended. I was no longer taking the physical beating of the job but was experiencing that awkward position of loss of control. My firefighters always did great work but I was the one held responsible if something went wrong and I was totally dependent on them to achieve success.

When I became a deputy chief I had arrived at the top of the pay scale but I had also reached the top of the stress pyramid. I was no longer supervising only four or five firefighters that I knew intimately. Now there were often more than a hundred people working at an incident, many of whom I didn't know at all, and all of whom I had to keep safe.

Stress on the fireground stemmed from a number of factors. First, there was the constant uncertainty. I had studied for years and was well versed in the strategy and tactics of managing a fire. However, there was always an endless range of unknowns at any incident. Substandard construction, illegal occupancies, hazardous building contents, and the vagaries of human behavior all led to unanticipated dangers. There is a science to firefighting but at times it is a very inexact science.

It was also a very complex job. Even a routine structural fire required initiating and managing a number of concurrent tasks. A water supply had to be established, hose lines stretched and operated, and searches for victims initiated. And all of these activities had to be carefully coordinated and timed in the proper sequence or people would be seriously injured. While all of this was going on you were constantly aware of the ticking clock. The longer it took to control the fire the more dangerous it became. There were many instances when it took a considerable amount of time just to locate the fire, especially in a commercial occupancy. I would often find myself standing in the street in front of a building that was spewing dense smoke without any visible fire showing and wondering just how much longer I could safely keep my firefighters working inside. Were they making progress? Did they need just a few more minutes to start attacking the fire? Or was the structure starting to weaken and was it time to pull everyone out to safety on the street? And if I chose that option was I abandoning some poor civilian who was trapped or overcome inside? These were heavy, life-and-death questions with no simple answers. The decision that was ultimately chosen, right or wrong, was mine and mine alone.

Somewhere back in Psychology 101 I had read that stress generally stems from feeling a loss of control. As a deputy chief I was in the awkward position of being the man in charge of an operation but I was unable to directly "control" much of that operation. No matter how urgently I wanted to get a hose line in operation, maneuver a ladder, or reposition a fire truck I could not do it myself. I had to order others to do it and the task always seemed to take forever. Firefighting is a brutally physical job and accomplishing any of these tasks took time—time that was always at a premium as the clock was constantly ticking in the back of my mind.

The most stressful part of the job occurred before I actually got to the scene of a fire. While responding in my chief's car I was usually bombarded by radio messages from the fire department dispatcher, snippets of transmissions from the firefighters' radios in the fire building, and the occasional cell phone call from someone who was sitting in a comfy office downtown. All of this went on against the background noise of emergency vehicle sirens and horns from the typically congested city traffic. It was actually a relief when I arrived at the job. Much like a prizefighter who finally gets to box after prolonged introductions, I could start functioning like a chief rather than feeling like someone listening in from the sidelines. I could visually size up the problems and begin to formulate a plan of action.

I soon learned some techniques that helped me handle the stress.

Sticking to my routines helped a lot. Each tour I worked I made sure to know which battalion chiefs were working and what level of competency I could expect from them. Fortunately I had a number of excellent veterans I could rely on. If the chief was newly pro-moted or someone I did not know at all, I would show up to work with a mindset to be far more "hands-on" in managing the fire until I got a clearer read on the chief's abilities. I fought off all the sensory distractions while I was still respond-ing in my vehicle and tried to focus on gathering in-formation about the fire building and recording the specific units assigned on the alarm. Keeping busy was not only productive, it also forged an escape from the tension of the work.

Quick, high-stakes decisions were often required based on limited or confusing information. The rank of deputy chief could be a very stimulating but stressful job (photograph by Bill Tompkins).

When the noise and onslaught of urgent mes-sages and other distractions on the fireground got overwhelming I learned that it was best to just walk away for a few seconds. If I stood alone a few feet removed from my command post I could gather my thoughts, get a more objective perspective of the problems, and, perhaps most important, relax a bit. In the past I had worked for some truly excellent chiefs. And I knew that a relaxed chief was a good incident commander. He could set the whole tone for a job and make you feel that, no matter how bad they seemed, the problems would ultimately be worked out.

If it was a really newsworthy event the mayor would eventually come to the scene to do his job of putting a public face on whatever disaster was at hand. It was no big hassle having him appear but I never got comfortable with his underlings. In particular, some of Rudy Giuliani's minions were hard to deal with. The mayor's impending arrival would often be heralded by an advanced wave of sharply dressed city hall subordinates who would arrive on scene with cell phones plastered to their ears and excitedly announce, "He's coming, he's coming!" followed by "He's here, he's here!" once he got there, as though his presence would in any way affect what my men and I were doing. I was immersed in the work of trying to manage the incident and found their presence an annoying distraction that just added to the stress level. I sometimes felt like grabbing them by their tailored Brooks Brothers lapels and asking why they needed to kowtow to this man. Couldn't they see that the mayor was just a man like everyone else who put his pants on one leg at a time? Did their politically appointed jobs mean so much to them that they were willing to submerge their pride in their blind adoration? But I'm sure that their bureaucratic minds would have rapidly dismissed my words as meaningless rants flowing from a disgruntled civil servant.

Regardless of how complex and challenging a fire turned out to be I found that I preferred to manage the incident on my own. Without the distraction of fire department superiors, city hall cronies, and representatives of other agencies I was able to concentrate on developing my skills as a deputy chief. Eventually I got better at seeing the big picture at a fire operation rather than focusing on individual small slices of the scenario. I began a path that would eventually make me a "harder" individual capable of handling the discomfort of being the man in charge.

And, yes, things eventually turned out well as I stood there sweating in that hospital lobby. I took a deep breath and reevaluated the situation. I forced myself to slow down and communicate with purpose and clarity. If I wasn't yet a confident incident commander I sure as hell was going to try and sound like one. And with some outstanding help from my firefighters the incident was safely resolved. When I walked out of that lobby, I was a little more experienced in commanding a fire and, just as significant, a bit more capable of handling my own stress.

Thinking Like an
Incident Commander

That hospital fire was different from the other operations I managed as brand new deputy chief since it had the potential to affect so many patients. But similar to the other fires I had experienced at that point, it was just one of numerous routine jobs that occurred each day in New York City. After working for two months in my new rank I was still anxiously awaiting the "Big One," the fire that would truly challenge my abilities and confront me with all the stresses, multi-faceted dangers, and difficult decisions that come with supervising a major, multiple-alarm incident. My anxiety lingered and the stress grew as I anxiously waited for it to happen. I would often drive to work thinking, "This could be the night."

Meanwhile, the upper echelons of the FDNY management were constantly lurking in the background watching every move I made on the fireground. This was not necessarily a bad thing since some of them were great to work for and seemed sincerely interested in training me and helping me to become a competent incident commander. One in particular, Donald Burns, was always very supportive whenever he showed up at one of my fires. Once the incident was over we would discuss the operation and he would offer some suggestions to keep in mind for future jobs. Donald was a great chief and an excellent mentor. Sadly, he was one of many who would die on 9/11.

Unfortunately, not all of my supervisors were like that. Although I started developing a good rapport with most of them, one in particular stood out, and not in a positive way. Phil Crusoe (most definitely not his real name) was, quite simply, a very difficult man. Overwhelmingly critical, chronically demanding, and impossible to please, he embodied just about all the characteristics of a really bad manager. He had a lot of time on the job and it seemed like he had spent those many years refining his difficult persona. Like all chiefs, Phil started out as a firefighter and had risen through the ranks to achieve his lofty position on the fire department totem pole. But somewhere in that process he seemed to have shed certain aspects of his humanity if indeed he had ever possessed them. I had worked for a number of great leaders and something they all had in common was a willingness to remember where they came from. Even the most highly ranked members of the department had once been struggling recruits, freshly minted company officers, and newly promoted chiefs and they understood the realities of the job. Phil, however, seemed to have been immaculately conceived in his upper management position. He was truly incapable of seeing any flaw in the unrealistic demands he put on his underlings and he did not hesitate to use his position to intimidate the people below him. Think Miranda Priestly from *The Devil Wears Prada* in a fire helmet. He was the ultimate control freak and demanded rigid compliance with his lofty requirements. Phil was a strict rule follower but he seldom came up with any creative ideas on his own. In short, he was the perfect civil service automaton intent on molding the job, and the world, into something he could control.

Needless to say, in a department rife with opinions about just about everybody in it, Phil did not have a great reputation. And the more I dealt with him the further my own opinion went in that same direction. He and I were the proverbial oil and water in philosophy, personality, management style, and temperament. It didn't take long for him to distrust me and eventually I felt the same toward him. Our work relationship seemed to evolve into more than just mutual dislike. We quickly became opponents locked in an ongoing, non-verbal but very real battle between supervisor and subordinate. I became his white whale and he was my Ahab.

At the start of every tour I would check and see who was working as the city-wide supervisor. If it was Phil I knew right away that it would be a long, difficult day and I could look forward to getting numerous phone calls from him regarding trivial corrections to routine reports and other aspects of pointless administrative esoterica. There were times when I couldn't believe that the city was paying me to do this stuff when there was so much more creative and important work I could accomplish on my own.

But the most trying moments of dealing with Phil occurred when he showed up at my fires. As the superior officer his role was to assume command of the job, evaluate the situation, and provide any needed support. There were city-wide supervisors who excelled at this. When they arrived on scene I would advise them of the strategy I had established and give a rundown on how my personnel were deployed. They would listen to me, make their own observations, and recommend any adjustments they felt were required. I always had a sense that they were there to assist me and everyone else at the scene to run the operation safely and efficiently. I'm sure that Phil intended to do the same but his methods usually led to increasing the stress levels in what was already a stressful situation. Just as he did when dealing with administrative matters he would evaluate and question every minute aspect of the job. But he never did this in a positive or helpful way. In fact, his recommendations were usually correct but his manner put everyone on edge. It was as if we were all being tested rather than supported, and his constant questioning of everything we did accomplished little more than to create a sense of always needing to look over your shoulder and wonder if you were doing the right thing. It often felt like I was wrestling with Phil as much as the fire itself. I wanted to tell him, "Please step back and just let me run the operation, and when it's all over we'll discuss it and then you can feel free to whip me." But in a quasi-military organization that was not an option.

One time during a meeting in his office Phil and I had a most revealing conversation. He was well aware of my fire department background. When I had been promoted to the deputy chief rank I had been on the job for 17 years, all of them in the field fighting fires as firefighter, company officer, and battalion chief. Over that time I had been to hundreds of fires and worked throughout the city at various assignments. I tried to learn something at every fire I went to and I had studied very hard for the promotional exams. Like many other people on the job I was highly motivated and was rewarded for my efforts.

To anyone outside of the FDNY 17 years might seem like a long time to be doing something, and in reality it was. However, by FDNY standards, most deputy chiefs had spent far more time on the job than I had. And on some deep level this seemed to really trouble Phil. During our talk he mentioned that I had "overcome all the obstacles to get to where I was," but it didn't come across at all in a positive way. What he was not saying, but certainly projecting, was more like "How dare you to have the audacity to overcome all those obstacles?" It was clear that, in his opinion, I didn't deserve the position.

While he couldn't come right out and say it, it had been laid out on the table. He didn't view me as a motivated, competent fire officer but as an interloper in his hollowed and exclusive world of fire department upper management. I had enough confidence in myself to know he was wrong but his opinion certainly explained the constant bombardment he had subjected me to both on the fireground and during our office meetings. It also explained why, behind my back, he had approached several of my coworkers to ask their opinion about my competency as a chief. I have no doubt that it further frustrated him that he could find no one who would say a bad word about me or my performance.

So the stage had been set and the plot had been written. Two months into the rank of deputy chief I was still anxiously anticipating the colossal, challenging fire I knew was somewhere out there just waiting for me. And among the cast of characters there was indeed one who had assumed the role of nemesis. Finally, during an early spring night the curtain went up.

If you take a moment to Google "church fires" you will find a long history of major incidents that often do not end very well. Words like "massive," "apocalyptic," and "gutted" regularly describe the events. A fire in a church is not only a difficult operation; it is also one that often results in a total loss of the building. There are a number of reasons for this. These fires often occur at night when the building is unoccupied and there is a delayed notification to the fire department. Naturally this allows more time for the fire to expand and intensify. And this is occurring in a structure that is likely to be very old, loaded with combustible material, and full of wide-open spaces that create ready paths for the fire and heat to travel.

It was about eight in the evening when I got the phone call from the dispatcher informing me that I had a "good job" going in a church. His choice of works said a lot since most of the time these calls merely relayed basic, detached facts about the building address and the units assigned to the incident. If the normally unflappable dispatcher described it as a good job I knew right away that something big was going on. I also knew that my buddy Phil was working. All of the elements for the perfect storm were in place. The "Big One" had finally arrived and the person I least wanted to be there was going to be present to complicate the challenge.

You would think that all of this would stress me out. Yet I felt an overwhelming sense of only one thing. And that was an enormous sense of relief. Finally, I was getting the opportunity to face the things I feared: to function as the incident commander of a significant and unusually challenging operation that would test me and require me to lead and make difficult fireground decisions. As I walked down the stairs to get to my car I was almost shocked to find that I was not the least bit nervous. In fact, I couldn't wait to get to the scene and begin to tackle the problem, to see what I was made of, to finally discover if this job was truly for me.

The fire was not that far away and I arrived at the scene in under five minutes. Sure enough, a major conflagration was in progress. Dark smoke was spewing from the roof of a large church that appeared to be about a hundred years old. There was a separate rectory building right next to it that also had fire showing in the basement and the upper floors. Apparently the fire had originated in the rectory and spread to the church and it all had grown rapidly before the fire department had even been notified. A burning church by itself would have been a significant challenge but now there were two separate building fires to manage. That meant a

An older church has the potential to produce a massive fire due to the size, contents, and open spaces inside the structure (photograph by Steve Spak).

lot of personnel performing numerous tactics would have to be supervised in different locations. And those tactics would have to be carefully coordinated and controlled so that the many firefighters at the scene did not interfere with each other's activities or injure each other. In short, someone had to make sure that an overall strategy was established and that someone was me.

Firefighting is an arduous and stressful job but much of it is not

Church fires do not always end well. Extensive damage is generally the norm (photograph by Bill Tompkins).

rocket science. Just as in dealing with any complicated challenge it often comes down to dividing a large, chaotic situation into smaller, more manageable sections. I immediately assigned battalion chiefs to supervise different areas of the two buildings, established lines of communication, and called for an additional alarm assignment to get more units and personnel to the scene. That was my logical side kicking in, getting the things in place that I needed as a starting point. But there is always an intuitive, subjective force at work in everything we do in life and that force is also present on the fireground. As I stood in front of the church I watched as my men worked quickly and efficiently and operated several hose lines at different locations. However, while all of this was being accomplished I continued to have a nagging feeling that none of it seemed right. The volume of fire, the color and pressure of the smoke, the amount of time we had been working, all the subtle signs that tell you that you're not making the progress you should be making started eating at my gut. And my gut was telling me that the ticking clock that was present at every emergency operation had been ticking at this one for too long, that it was time to get out, to withdraw my men from the buildings, to place them in safe positions and attack the fire from the outside. As I ordered them back out to the street I initiated a roll call to make sure everyone was accounted for and started setting up the heavy caliber streams that would knock down the fire from the exterior.

In a heartbeat I had completely changed the entire strategy from an aggressive, interior attack on the fire to a defensive, exterior approach from the street. It was really less a logical decision and more an intuitive reaction to what I was sensing. And that reaction stemmed from both the images that were planted in my head from many previous fires along with the example that the chiefs I had worked for in the past had set for me. And most certainly the memory of rushing out of a collapsing Harlem tenement back when I was a captain had been etched in my mind.

I remember feeling a combination of both relief and satisfaction as we renewed our assault on the fire—relief because I had removed people from danger and satisfaction because I had not been afraid to pull the trigger and make a key decision, a decision that anyone aspiring to be an incident commander would have to make. And it proved to be the right decision. Afterward one of my battalion chiefs asked me what I had observed that made me order a change in strategy. In reality it had less to do with what I saw and more with what I *felt*. I was learning to trust my intuition, a skill that would help me many times in my career.

After knocking down much of the heavy flames from the exterior we were able to safely position men back inside to completely extinguish the fire and perform the necessary searches. Rather than becoming yet another disastrous example you could look up on Google, the church is still in use today.

By the time Phil arrived at the scene we had a handle on the fire. As usual, before he even went over to speak to me, he walked around to evaluate the job and, for once, was hard pressed to find anything wrong with the strategy or any detail that needing his personal correction. With some quick decision making, and a lot of good support from the firefighters performing the work, it had been a textbook operation. I'm sure that as he was responding to a multiple alarm for an advanced fire in a church Phil had anticipated having a disaster on his hands. Instead, he was met with a carefully controlled, well-run fire.

A curious thing happened when Phil and I finally had a chance to speak. I saw him from a distance and, as our eyes met, we both smiled. But if you could read the subtleties of the gesture it wasn't really like a smile of camaraderie. I think that behind his grin Phil was thinking something like "Dunne, this went pretty well. You may not be as incompetent as I thought." And hidden by my smile was "Screw you, Phil. I can do this job and do it well despite you and your constant irritating interference." Ahab had not befriended the whale but was at least starting to show a level of acceptance.

I later heard through the grapevine that Phil had raved to some other people about how well things had gone at my church fire. But he never said a word to me about it. At first I felt frustrated about not getting any positive feedback at all. But, in retrospect, I'd have to say that there was a certain purity to the way things went. For Phil to have offered me any effusive complements would have been totally out of character for him. That would been kind of like a Hamlet who could actually make a decision, a Willie Lowman who was not deluded, or a Superman who was immune to kryptonite. Instead, he stayed true to form. He may have been a pain in the butt but he would remain a predicable pain in the butt.

However, this fire was a benchmark in both my relationship with Phil and my ability as an incident commander. Much as I had discovered years earlier in my probie school smoke house experience, the fear of an unknown challenge turned out to be far worse than the reality. When I had this church fire I couldn't have imagined all the fires, and nightmares, that awaited me and the FDNY in the years to come. I learned with each fire or disaster I went to and despite all the obstacles, or perhaps because of all the obstacles, playing the role of being the guy in charge eventually became one of my most fulfilling job experiences.

There are times when I wonder how all of this exposure to chaos and devastation has affected my perspective on life. I have left that line of work but the essence of being an incident commander remains deeply embedded in my psyche. I have learned to look at the world not as it exists in its pristine state but as a fragile existence that is to be totally enjoyed in the moment, for the potential disaster always is just a heartbeat away. And just as I can look at a brand-new car and envision the scratches and dents that await it in the future, I have a healthy respect for the dangers that lurk in everyday life. When I see a construction crane in mid–Manhattan I can imagine the extent of the damage that will occur if it collapses. When I get on a plane or go into a theatre I do check for the location of the exits. And, of course, I sometimes look at a building and can't help but wonder where a fire might break out and how I could contain it.

However, it isn't all just negative paranoia that I'm left with. On the contrary, I drew a great deal of positive input from all of those years of being a fireground commander. That background has also implanted the confidence and optimism to know that, no matter how overwhelming any challenge or danger may seem, you can always step back, plan a course of action, and use your intuition to overcome it. And isn't that a great skill to have in life?

On the Circuit

After a few years of managing fires and emergencies I found my comfort zone. I had come a long way from those first uncertain and nerve-racking experiences of being the man in charge and settled into a position in the department I had never envisioned myself being in. Back when I was a firefighter or company officer I viewed a deputy chief as someone that I really didn't want to be around. And I certainly wasn't comfortable if he visited my firehouse because he was so high up in the department bureaucracy. What was he looking for? What would he want? (My discomfort with authority was no doubt a remnant of childhood school days, a good part of which were spent awaiting the inevitable physical assault or aggressive interrogation that certain members of "religious" orders considered an integral part of a good education.) Most of the deputy chiefs were OK guys but in truth how many of us really want the big boss around? Now I was one of them and had an appreciation for both the trials and the rewards of being in the upper echelons of the FDNY. But there was another kind challenge I was curious about.

The fire service, just like any other industry, holds conventions throughout the country. Thousands of firefighters attend to hear lectures and numerous private vendors come to market their safety equipment. It's a big business that draws some of the most noteworthy leaders in the rarified world of firefighting. I wanted to try jumping into that arena myself. Primarily I wanted to test myself as a public speaker but, yes, there was also some ego involved (which I suspect is a motivator for a lot of what we do in life).

I was comfortable conducting a drill in a firehouse kitchen. But that usually involved speaking to a group of only about a dozen or so individuals, many of whom I already knew. Presenting at one of the conventions would involve lecturing to a room full of 200 or more people I had never met. I found the thought of that kind of terrifying. How could I possibly perform before such an assembly and hold their interest for two or more hours?

One of my coworkers was already a nationally known speaker on the convention circuit and I decided to attend one of his lectures. I wasn't really interested in what he taught, I just wanted to get a sense of his approach and how he handled the audience. After his presentation we spoke and I told him what I was trying to do. His only advice was to just be myself.

I thought about that a bit. What in all honesty did it mean to be myself? I knew that I had the necessary intelligence and motivation. But I also knew that my vocal cords were not that strong. Nor did I have an especially melodious voice. I could sing in the shower but might have a hard time projecting in a large lecture room. And I was not blessed with Daniel Webster–like oratory skills. But when I perused the roster of people who had lectured at one of the conventions, I noted that none of them had anywhere near the actual fireground experience that I possessed. I had worked in some of the busiest areas of the most active fire department in the country. Surely that would count for something. I had been inside a lot of burning buildings and commanded scores of challenging, stressful incidents as a chief. How much more difficult could it be to stand up in a lecture hall where the ceiling was not about to collapse and people were not dying and the worst that could happen would be a computer malfunction? Besides, I had learned that the best reaction to what seemed like an uncomfortable experience was to not overanalyze the thing and just throw myself into it.

So I started to prepare my lectures and quickly learned that much of the art of a good presentation was in the ability to provide relevant information in elaborate gift wrapping. And that led to an introduction to the perils of PowerPoint. For better or for worse that particular computer program has become the deus ex machina of the modern lecture. It is hard to overestimate the extent of its influence. As Christopher Brownfield pointed out in his book *My Nuclear Family*, "Military historians can debate at length which innovation in technology has had the second greatest effect on modern warfare, but it is undisputed that the PowerPoint presentation takes the prize for first."

Unfortunately, my computer skills at the time were stuck somewhere in the middle of the Stone Age. So I hustled off to the library and took out a book about effective PowerPoint presentations. And I got as far as page four before I put it down in utter boredom. I found that it was much better just to learn by trial and error and started playing around with the program. However, my technology-challenged soul was quickly overwhelmed by the vagaries of computer minutia. There were so many options to weigh. Did I want my information to just appear on a slide or have each line artfully zip in one bullet at a time? Should I have a basic slide to slide transition or should each new one drop down dramatically from the top or side of the screen? What were the most eye-catching videos and sound bites? I wanted to be entertaining but not cute, informative but not sleep inducing, and occasionally humorous but not slapstick. My goal was to teach an audience, not to be the host of *The Tonight Show*. Still, an important aspect of presenting was not only the factual information but also the "show" that goes with it.

Eventually I learned not to follow the dictates of PowerPoint too closely. The preprogrammed templates were designed to produce slides that were loaded with numerous bullets and tons of information. In short, they created presentations that were overwhelming and boring. What I had to do was to make myself and my stories the focus of a lecture with the projection screen playing a mere background role.

The first time I lectured before a large audience was at a convention in Atlantic City, New Jersey. The organization running the event fixed me up with a room on an upper floor of a high-rise casino that was located right on the boardwalk with an awesome view of the ocean. I was enjoying that vista while I got dressed and was preparing to leave for the convention hall. As I was redoing my tie for the second or third time (I wanted to look "professional" and had to get it just right) I glanced out of the window and saw a school of dolphins frolicking in the nearby surf. Being city-born and city-raised, I was fascinated by the sight of these animals swimming so close to a busy urban beach. Now I was really excited. Here I was about to address a large group of people for the first time and I had also been treated to an unexpected sight. Necktie in place and laptop in hand, I rushed down to the lobby to tell somebody about the amazing sight I had just witnessed.

The hotel lobby was a gambling casino about the size of a football field. The room had no sense of time, weather, or anything else pertaining to the outside world, just the constant drone of games of chance and a cloud of cigarette smoke that banked down nearly to the floor. I rushed up to the first group I encountered, several elderly people who were mechanically staring at their slot machines. With zealot-like enthusiasm, I began to regale them with my *National Geographic* moment. Slowly, they lifted their bloodshot eyes from the slots, stared blankly at me, and then quickly moved away to more distant machines. Two security guards cautiously approached and eyed me nervously. Faced with an underwhelming response to my dolphin story, I started heading to the convention center for my lecture.

There was supposed to be a regularly scheduled bus running from the hotel to the convention hall. But, of course, as I nervously paced in the hotel lobby, it never came at all and so, with time running short, I decided to walk. And, of course, as soon as I was halfway into my walk it started to rain. My recently purchased, neatly pressed light blue dress shirt suddenly became a somewhat rumpled light blue shirt covered with numerous raindrop-inspired polka dots. Now I really started feeling nervous. I was experiencing performance anxiety about the lecture, I looked totally disheveled despite my obsessive grooming, and behind it all the clock was ticking and I wasn't even sure if I was going to get there on time.

I did finally arrive at the convention hall, slightly breathless and on time. I think the room I was assigned to was called the "Miss America Ball Room" or something like that (Atlantic City did have its share of schmaltz). There were already about a hundred people waiting in line to register for the lecture and enter the room. I felt a bit awkward and didn't know exactly what to do before the session began so I decided to stand at the entrance door and greet the attendees as they came in. I'm not sure if I felt more like a maître d' greeting patrons at a restaurant or a funeral director gently welcoming the bereaved—there were probably elements of both going on in my brain.

Finally everyone was seated and, after one final adjustment to my tightly knotted tie and a subtle check to insure that my fly was zipped all the way up, I proceeded to the front of the room. Once I got up there I started talking and being myself, just as my coworker had recommended. Much to my relief I felt very relaxed and found that I actually enjoyed what I was doing. It was kind of like going to a fire. On the job I would experience a lot of anxiety while I was responding in but always felt a calm sense of control once I arrived at the scene. And much like orchestrating a fire operation I found that I could lead, prod, evaluate, and communicate with this mass of people I was addressing. The group had a chemistry of its own and it was kind of thrilling to sense their feedback while I spoke about my topic and tried to present my information in an entertaining manner.

In two hours it was all over. After the session I could tell from the comments of people who came up to speak to me along with a perusal of the student evaluations that they had liked the lecture. I had pulled it off! Essentially I did what I had done on the fireground dozens of times—I had *acted* confidently even though I hadn't felt all that confident.

I eventually developed a real sense of ease as a public speaker and got to lecture throughout the country to both firefighter and civilian audiences. Traveling to the various conventions was an experience in itself and provided an interesting sideline to my main job as a fire chief. The trips quickly became somewhat routine. They all started out in the same way, which is to say with me standing in the TSA line at the airport. Burdened with my suit coat, laptop, and luggage I would join my fellow travelers in the ritual of mass disrobing as we removed coats, hats, belts, and shoes to display our innocence of terrorist intent. Even though I knew I was a completely unthreatening passenger I always felt an odd desire to gratefully and pathetically hug a TSA agent when I finally got through the whole process. There was an illogical sense of relief that I had once again passed inspection. It was as if on some subconscious level I must be guilty of *something* and the screening devices I passed through were capable of unveiling my most intimate fantasies or revealing the overly creative deductions I took on my last tax return.

I traveled to a lot of areas throughout the country and always took the time to explore the town that was hosting the convention. The local accents, the food, and the architecture might change but regardless of where I was it was always obvious when a firefighting convention was in town. I could spot a firefighter a mile away. There were often groups of them walking around the city exploring the sites and perusing the bars, all dressed in their identical navy blue fire department t-shirts. It was kind of neat to see the pride they took in being a member of their particular organization. Being a firefighter was a vital part of their identity and their shirts proudly proclaimed their membership in places like the Long Grove, Iowa, or East McKeesport, Pennsylvania, volunteer fire departments. It must have been a male bonding kind of thing; I just can't envision a group of women being equally at ease with each other if they were all dressed in identical Versace outfits.

The conventions that were geared for a civilian audience were different. Since they didn't wear uniforms they kind of blended in with the normal business and tourist crowds. And while they also enjoyed socializing and sightseeing they tended to do it in a far less boisterous way. The civilians seemed to attend these events as individuals while the firefighters viewed them as exercises in brotherhood and they weren't shy about enjoying themselves in a bar or restaurant. The business owners liked them since they brought exuberant life, and a lot of money, to their establishments.

However, I saw certain things in common whether I lectured at a civilian or firefighter convention. There would always be one or two people in the audience who would stare at their cell phones nonstop throughout my presentation. It was as if they were heads of state of a small country and the possibility of missing even one email could lead to disastrous consequences. There was also the occasional "sleeper," usually a firefighter who had had a hard night or an overly indulgent evening and had difficulty keeping his eyes open. And I don't mean for just a few minutes of rest but for the *entire* session. On some level I was envious of their ability to be so comfortable with enjoying the immediate gratification of sleep while remaining totally oblivious of how it affected the people around them. I would try not to let it bother me, to tell myself that they *were* just a few individuals and that the vast majority of the audience was listening to what I was saying. But, try as I may, I couldn't help but continually look at them and wonder how long they would actually sleep or see at what point the cell phone addicts would actually move their eyes away from their screens.

But overall the people in my audiences were usually courteous and actively participated in my lectures. I didn't like to stand in one spot when I spoke and would usually move around to engage different segments of the room. Some attendees liked this and others probably found it annoying. As I "worked" the room it occurred to me that there must be an entire science dedicated to studying exactly where people choose to sit in a lecture hall. Those who sat right up front seemed to take copious notes and were more likely to ask questions. The back row crowd was less likely to get involved in the class and seemed to relish their distance from the speaker as well as their ability to subtly exit the room in the event they became disinterested (I know this because I tend to sit in the back row when I attend a lecture).

I always welcomed questions and generally got some well-thought-out inquiries that led to good discussions. But just as I had learned to manage a fire operation, I also learned how to manage an audience. There was the occasional long-winded "question" that was more of a soliloquy from someone who was primarily interested in displaying the extent of his knowledge to the other people in the room. Such public expressions of ego can be awkward and annoying and I tried to seek input from the more introverted audience members to balance out those who would otherwise dominate the room.

As I was learning the intricacies of group dynamics I was also discovering that unless you were a celebrity or an ex-president you would never get rich on the lecture circuit. And that was fine by me since I had a regular job that I liked and had not ventured into the speaking world with the intent of becoming rich. Some events would pay me a moderate speaking fee, others might barely cover my travel expenses. And while some were rather informal in nature others required strict adherence to a series of requirements that made me feel like I was joining the Marine Corps. Following is an actual agreement required by one of my conventions. I have conservatively edited it and liberally commented on it in brackets:

The Presenter [i.e., me] *hereby irrevocably permits and authorizes the conference to display, publicly perform, exhibit, transmit, broadcast, reproduce, record, photograph, digitize, modify, alter, edit, adapt,... exploit* [interesting choice of words], *sell, and rent the presentation on a perpetual basis* [that's a long time] *throughout the world* [that's a lot of territory] *in any medium of format whatsoever now existing or hereafter created* [perhaps a hologram may someday be performing one of my lectures?].... *All rights not specifically granted to the convention are reserved to the Presenter* [I am hard pressed to come up with any rights that are left to me other than the right to remain silent. At least they didn't ask for possession of my firstborn child].

The funny thing is, when I did speak at that particular convention, the individuals who ran it were very supportive and were some of the easiest-going people I have ever worked with. Perhaps there are just too many underemployed law school graduates out there.

Someone once suggested to me that the real business of these events is about sales and that the speakers are just the dog and pony show designed to attract people to come to the convention and purchase the safety products that are displayed by the vendors. Having had so many great interactions with bright, motivated people in my lectures, I think that is entirely too cynical an outlook. But if I am wrong about that I do hope that my dog and pony at least put on a good performance.

The Lie

The man had obviously been in the process of painting his Bronx apartment. But now he was dead and lying face down in a small bathroom surrounded by several cans of paint thinners and other volatile fluids. There was something eerily familiar about the body and as I stood over it I flashed back for a brief moment to another victim I had seen years ago in Brooklyn. The fire marshals would be coming to the scene to perform an investigation but all indications were that one tiny, ill-timed spark had ignited the room as he was working and suddenly ended his life.

Whoever he was, he was not a young man. I examined the burns to his flesh and clothing and noted how, once again, fire had transformed a breathing, feeling person into a lifeless mass of damaged tissue devoid of any sense of his previous humanity. But that was only a fleeting thought as I proceeded to mentally record the facts I needed to extract from the scene.

An extensive and detailed report was required whenever there was a fire fatality and, unfortunately, over the years I had prepared far too many of them. However, this particular one looked like it wouldn't be too complicated. There was only one victim this time, not several of them. And though you didn't want anyone to die, at least there were no children involved. I even had favorable conditions in which to perform my investigative work. It was daytime and the apartment was well lit and I didn't have the physical challenge of slogging through knee-deep fire debris or a flooded basement as I had so often in the past.

I proceeded to gather facts, take measurements, and make observations. It was always kind of odd to be doing this while working around a corpse but over the years I had grown accustomed to it. As I walked throughout the apartment, and around the dead body, I recorded the room dimensions, noted the presence of smoke detectors, and evaluated the victim's location. Sometimes the body itself could provide a clue. Things as subtle as the direction it was facing and whether it was found in a face up or prone position might prove to be relevant. And as I did my work I had to treat that body not as a person but as another item to be considered in uncovering the facts of this incident just as I would analyze the fire's point of origin or any other piece of evidence. I moved around the ruins of the apartment, past shattered windows and soot-covered walls, and performed a detached calculus of a dead man who, just an hour earlier, had relished this place as his private sanctuary. But I gave no thought to what his life had been like or what kind of person he was or who he may have loved when he was alive. I was not looking to reconstruct the essence of the man but to understand the scenario that had killed him.

It hadn't always been that way. The first fatality I had seen, as a brand new probie, wasn't at a fire but at an automobile accident. I can still remember seeing the man slumped behind the wheel of his car. He looked surprisingly undamaged and had an almost peaceful air about him as though he had paused to take a nap rather than having just experienced a violent end to his life. It was the sad and sudden finality of that death that left me thinking about him for some time after. Here was a young man who had been driving a car just as I did on a street that I myself had often used. Now he was simply gone in a permanent and inexplicable way while the other firefighters and I continued to work around him, breathing air, talking, thinking, and living our lives. I wondered about all of the factors that had fallen into place to create the sad circumstances that ended his existence. What if he had simply turned the wheel a little more to the right or driven a bit slower or just delayed his trip by a minute? Then he would be walking around like the rest of us and his family would not be getting the horrendous phone call they were about to receive.

I remained perplexed by this stunning transition from life to utter nonexistence for some time. About two years later I saw a burn victim at a fire in Manhattan. Despite the fact that large areas of his skin were peeling off the man was walking around conversing with people and acting like nothing had happened. The burns had destroyed his nerve cells and the shock of his injury thankfully kept him free of pain. The day after the fire I ran into the chief who had been in charge and asked him how the guy was doing. This particular chief had been on the job for almost 40 years and had an impressive reputation. I expected to hear that the victim was still recovering in the hospital. But the chief informed me that he had died and explained that when someone lost that amount of skin, very often he didn't survive. The chief had an extensive background and had obviously seen this many times in the past. I, on the other hand, was still relatively new to this line of work and it was hard for me to accept the fact that I had just seen the man moving around rather freely and looking much more like a survivor than like someone who was on the verge of dying. I liked the idea that our job involved rescuing people but I hadn't quite yet come to terms with the fact that, despite our efforts, some people were destined to die. That was certain to change. The Happy Land Social Club fire, 9/11, and a lot of other experiences were yet to come.

A few years and three promotions later I found myself working as a battalion chief. My firefighting resume had grown but despite my added experience, on some deep level I still harbored elements of shock and awe whenever I encountered a fire victim. I was becoming a good fire officer but hadn't totally refined the ability to maintain the emotional distancing this line of work required. I had not yet become sufficiently "fire hard-ened." Looking back I can't help but wonder if that was necessarily a bad thing.

However, as far as the job was concerned, whatever level of sensitivity I still possessed was entirely irrelevant in my new position as a battalion chief. I had a job to do and I had to do it in many different areas of the city. One night I was sent to work in Brooklyn and experienced my first fatal fire working as a chief. When I entered the apartment I saw the man lying face down in the bathroom. I remember feeling really bad for the guy as I gazed at his severely burned corpse. But a lot more had happened than I initially realized. The investigating fire marshals quickly determined that he had intentionally started the fire himself, most likely for insurance pur-poses. They also arrested his wife who had been standing by in the street. The burn marks on her clothing, combined with other pieces of evidence, suggested that she had also been involved in the crime.

It was a harsh reminder of the dark reality that sometimes surfaced on the job. I would often encounter victims. But occasionally I would also uncover people who were driven by anger or greed. People who were capable of totally ignoring the moral consequences of their actions. As I stood in that small room and stared at the man's fire-ravaged body I felt somewhat amazed that he had done all of this just for financial gain. A home had been destroyed, dozens of firefighters had been put at risk, neighboring buildings were affected, and this one man was responsible for it all. His actions had led to nothing but damage to others and a horren-dous end for himself.

In death he looked much like the victim I would encounter years later as a deputy chief in the Bronx. Both were middle-aged men of similar stature, each had been severely burned, and their bodies were lying in the exact same position on the floor of a small bathroom surrounded by the silent devastation that lingered after all fires. It made sense that one would so closely remind me of the other and that the sight of the dead man in the Bronx would bring an immediate flashback to the man in Brooklyn. It was like the physical evidence hadn't changed much in the 20 years that separated the two incidents. What had changed was within me. All those years as a chief had certainly affected my outlook. When I investigated the Bronx fatality I was able to accomplish the task in a much more detached manner than I would have 20 years earlier. My "hardening process" no doubt had a growth spurt that night in Brooklyn.

As soon as I finished sketching out the details of the Bronx victim I headed back downstairs to the street. We were in the "overhaul" stage of the operation, a painstaking process of thoroughly and systematically opening up the walls and ceilings to assure that no hidden pockets of fire remained. Because there had been a fatality the work had to be carefully controlled so that any remaining physical evidence would not be compromised.

I continued to monitor the overhaul work and made the required notifications to headquarters about the particulars of the fatality. At the same time I mentally prepared myself to face the radio and television reporters that would be drawn to the scene. This was always a bit of a balancing act since I wanted to provide them with accurate facts about the incident without compromising the privacy of the victim or the integrity of the ongoing investigation.

While I was in the middle of all this activity a middle-aged woman rapidly approached the command post. This was unusual since the police were usually good about controlling the crowds that gathered and giving us the room we needed to do our work. She seemed to know that I was the guy in charge and came right up to me. It was obvious that she was very upset about something and my immediate assumption was that she lived in one of the rooms below the fire and had water dripping from her ceilings or some other fire-related issue. That occurred all the time and I was prepared to politely request that she return to the other side of the police barricade for her own safety while I assigned a firefighter to check out her apartment. So I was totally unprepared for what came next. She told me that she lived in the apartment that had burned and wanted to know where her husband was.

I didn't know what to say. I was trained to fight fires, supervise emergencies, and analyze scenarios from a chief's perspective. I had been to a ton of disasters, fought a lot of fires, and dealt with the aftermath of a horrendous terrorist attack. But this was virgin territory for me. I had never before been placed in a position where I had to inform someone about an enormous personal loss. As she stood there looking so visibly distraught I was bursting with the knowledge that her husband was dead, knowledge that would absolutely devastate her. My mind still held fresh images of his burnt body lying on the bathroom floor and I felt conflicted and uncertain of what to say. I was pretty good at saving lives but rather inexperienced in reassuring survivors. And on top of it all I still had the distraction of supervising a fire operation. Do I just give her the horrible news and then pass her on to someone else or would that be entirely too abrupt? Might it ease her shock if I gently asked that she stand aside for now while I tried to gather more information (and my own composure)?

I knew that I had to say *something*, and in that mere second I had available to reach deep down inside my gut, I chose not to tell her. I lied and said that I just didn't know about her husband's status right now and then handed her over to some EMS personnel who were standing nearby. It just didn't seem right to put her in the position of being informed of her loss in a public setting. At least that was part of it. The truth is that I was also very uncomfortable with the thought of doing it myself. Had I gotten better at being a chief but worse at being a person?

Looking back I'm still not sure what my prime motivation was in handling it the way I did. I wonder if my discomfort with informing her may have possibly helped in some way and if some police officer or someone with more professional experience in these things gave her the bad news in a far better manner than I could have. At least that is my hope but I realize that may just be a means of reassuring myself that I did the right thing.

Nearly 20 years separated the Brooklyn and Bronx fires. But they had a lot in common. The men who died were about the same age and were similar in appearance and each had wives who were nervously pacing in the nearby streets. The big difference is that one of them was in the process of trying to improve the home he lived in while the other was trying to destroy his home for profit. And the other difference was me. I was not the same incident commander in Brooklyn that I was in the Bronx. Nor was I the same individual. Twenty years of this work had made me a good chief and, by necessity, a different person. But I wonder if in the process of becoming that person I had lost something and if a hardening of the emotions is just as much of a job hazard as a hardening of the arteries.

Zen and the Art
of Firefighting

I had been in the hospital room for hours. And though now I had left it, the sadness still clung to me like a wet overcoat that weighed me down emotionally and physically. My brother was dying, that much was certain, and there was nothing I could do but watch him as he laid unconscious on a hospital bed surrounded by his friends and coworkers, all of whom were strangers to me.

The news of his condition had come abruptly and painfully, a sudden phone call from Washington, D.C. *Your brother has cancer. His condition is grave, and you must come right away.* And I did come immediately, to a city I didn't know, to people I had never met, to my brother who could no longer communicate with me, and to the harsh realization that anything and everything I ever shared with him was over and done, in the past, and never to be experienced again.

Now I found myself standing in the waiting area of a restaurant after a long walk from the hotel I was staying in. Though the emotional burden had deadened my appetite I knew I had to continue to function, to go through the motions of eating even if I didn't feel like it. Given my mindset I certainly didn't feel like sitting down to eat in a crowded and festive restaurant and I had asked for my food to go so I could try to pick through it back in my room.

As I stood there waiting for my order I was struck by the glaring contrast between the lively, happy atmosphere of the restaurant and the somber environment of my brother's hospital room just a short distance away. I thought of him and of meals we had shared in places exactly like this and of the dismal reality of his condition. He would never, ever be able to do what everyone else was doing here. He would not eat a meal, go for a walk, hang out with friends, or leave the confines of the hospital.

And then I wasn't thinking at all. Perhaps it was the fatigue, the sor-

134

row, or the alienation but for whatever reasons I no longer held on to any thoughts, good or bad. I just started experiencing. The restaurant was the only tangible and present reality and for brief moments I found myself immersed in the immediacy of its atmosphere. I felt engulfed in the life and spirit of the place, the loud conversations, the backdrop of flickering television screens, the clatter of plates and cutlery, all of it punctuated by occasional bursts of joyous laughter. For a moment I let go of all the painful thoughts of my brother and I found myself experiencing the simple act of being in a restaurant in a way I had never experienced before. It was as if I had never been in a restaurant. I was not at all concerned with the food, or the menu, or the sports events on the TV screens. I was not hungry or concerned with how long I had to wait or distracted by the background noise. It was kind of a strange way to be in a restaurant, sort of out of it, not really caring, not judging the merits or the flaws of the place. I was simply *there*.

In my experience such unadorned, unanalyzed Zen-like moments have been rare. So those brief instances that allowed me to be released from the frantic stream of daily life and my normal means of perceiving the world were all the more striking when they did occur. I had a fleeting perception of that feeling as I waited in that Washington restaurant and on occasion I had such moments on my job. There was, for example, a red rose that would capture my focus when I looked through the windows of my Bronx office. The neighboring yard was covered with cement walkways and was tightly surrounded by gray tenements but it did have a tiny, struggling rose bush with one brilliant red flower that had somehow managed to blossom in the hostile environment. I looked at that rose for months. It managed to keep its color even into the cold weather and as I viewed it all of the office distractions just disappeared. My mind could turn off the constantly ringing phones and the nonstop background noise of the department radio with its endless chatter from the dozens of fire units that communicated on it.

In a similar manner I once observed a sparrow that happened to perch on my windowsill on one brutally cold day in an old, run-down Harlem firehouse. When I first saw it I thought about why such creature would choose to live in this drab place when it was free to go anywhere. Then I stopped questioning and just started sensing its nervous intensity and exuberant energy, and for a moment one human and one animal just experienced each other. There were other times when I found myself sitting in a firehouse kitchen sipping coffee and mindlessly gazing out at the trucks as they sat idly on the apparatus floor. There was a certain symmetry and reassurance in seeing the massive engine and ladder vehicles parked sliently next to each other. The engine with its neatly folded rows of hose lengths and the truck covered with clean ladders, hooks, and tools. There was an essential beauty in the simplicity of their design and in the way that the two rigs complemented each other in form and function. For at least a few seconds they could cease to be vehicles and just become shining images.

Such moments were calming and refreshing. They served as a reminder that there was a world beyond the harsh task of firefighting. And I felt more prepared to tackle that task after a few seconds of such contemplation. Yet those moments were by their very nature essentially at odds with the demands of my work. There was a clear dichotomy between the requirements of emergency awareness and the peace of Zen-like consciousness. As a fire chief I had to maintain a broad perspective of an emergency scenario and think of all the big picture ramifications as opposed to focusing on the minutia of one individual element. I was trained to consider complex fire situations rather than entertain simple concepts. And those situations demanded that I plan strategies and think of what might happen in a future timeframe rather that focus on the here and now. And throughout an operation, I had to evaluate and interpret the sights and sounds of a fire, to judge the intensity of the flames, the characteristics of the smoke, and the condition of my men, all of which was contrary to just being in the here and now and observing without really intellectualizing. The simplicity of the here-and-now perspective was a luxury not afforded to someone in a life-and-death profession.

There were brief moments on the fireground when that dichotomy became very apparent. Shortly after the 9/11 attack I found myself walking alone in the basement of one of the remaining Trade Center complex buildings. The structure had been damaged but much of the interior stood relatively unaffected. Several of the stores in the basement were left open and abandoned with virtually no trace of the catastrophic events that had occurred above. It was as if all of the commuters and shoppers had simply walked away. The normally crowded shops were eerily vacant and the merchandise just sat quietly beneath sales signs that no one would ever read. I had the place to myself and it was rather spooky. As I walked on I could see light reflecting on the back wall of a clothing store. Something was burning in the stockroom and for a few seconds I found myself fascinated by the orange images that were projected by the nearby flames. For those few moments there was no Trade Center tragedy to think of, just a brief and somewhat mesmerizing vision of those dancing colors as they flashed all over that wall. Then, suddenly and forcefully, I snapped back into the mindset of a fire chief who had to think, act, and evaluate rather than someone who could savor the experience of merely being a focused observer of life. In a heartbeat I felt the unnerving reality of the bizarre scenario. Here was a fire, burning in an open but totally abandoned public area, which would normally call for an instant response for firefighters to handle. Instead, it just flickered away unattended and seemingly irrelevant in contrast with the chaos and destruction of the streets above. For a brief moment I had been able to remove all peripheral concerns and just *see* this subterranean fire. But once that moment passed I realized, again, that this was indeed a scary place to be.

Fire was like that. It could fascinate and kill at the same time. With a certain perspective you could see its beauty just as you could sense its danger. There was something primal about it yet there was also something almost personal in the experience, especially if you were viewing it by yourself.

That was exactly what I encountered on one occasion in a burning building in the Bronx. I was crawling down a hallway in that building trying to determine exactly where the fire was located. That was not always an easy task in an era when thermal imaging cameras were not routinely available. Visible fire was a good thing—you could see it and get a sense of what you were dealing with. It was the hidden fire that most worried me, those cautious, nerve-wracking minutes when I groped through the darkness, uncertain of where the fire was and how advanced and dangerous it had become. The thermal imaging devices that are used today provide a good visual indication of heat sources on an electronic screen. When I was a truck officer I didn't have this tool and had to rely on my senses to interpret the subtle language of fire. Was the smoke changing in color and pressure as I crawled forward? Was the heat I felt on my ears or neck intensifying as I moved, indicating that I was getting close? And, always, in the back of my mind, was I pushing it too far, was I being too aggressive in my search and getting too distant from the safe location of the hose line? These were difficult questions to process. Firefighting was not a black and white occupation; it had a lot of uncertainties, a number of gray areas.

I was in that gray area when I crawled down that Bronx hallway. As I moved blindly beneath a layer of thick black smoke I could feel the heat banking down and sensed that I was getting close. And then, suddenly, looking through the plastic face piece of my mask I could see it lurking in the corner of a small room. The fire was just beyond the "incipient" stage. It had reached that point where it was no longer a harmless, newborn entity but a force that was growing in power and increasing its appetite. You could sense that it was primed to enlarge but there was no air movement to feed the oxygen it needed to rapidly spread. It just sat there in front of me, almost serenely, dancing very quietly inside the room with only an occasional soft snapping sound as it found new fragments of dry wood to consume. I laid there for a moment watching it, just me and one of the classic Greek elements, staring each other down.

As I viewed the fire for that brief moment it seemed like a mesmerizing presence, a state of existence as real and as legitimate as my own. I didn't view it as something good or bad, threatening or destructive. It just *was*. I had been to many fires but had never really *looked* at a fire in this way. And I felt privileged to observe it all by myself in those final few seconds before the engine company attacked it with the hose line and blasted it into a steamy white oblivion. I had done my job and done it well but had I also experienced that "Kenshō" moment that Zen seekers speak of? Had I known that same moment for an instant as I waited in that Washington restaurant, weighed down with upset and concern for my brother?

I have read that it takes a third of a second for the human brain to interpret a sensory experience. Perhaps a key to calming ourselves in a frantic world (and in a stressful occupation) is to develop the ability to stretch out that initial moment, to just see something and not try to explain or interpret it, to come face to face with existence free from cultural conditioning or preconceptions and just be in the here and now.

Of course, any prolonged immersion into such a mindset would have been irresponsible and dangerous in my line of work. And I never shared these thoughts with any of my coworkers. I was in a profession with no tolerance for such navel gazing. Still, though you will never read about it any firefighting textbook, I am convinced that the ability to slow down, turn off the distractions, and see things in a different light leads to a calmer mind. And a calmer mind is capable of making better decisions. And whether you are a plumber, a firefighter, or the president of the United States who couldn't benefit from that?

The Write Stuff

Perhaps this is a good point to talk about the process of writing this book. Just a few years ago the thought of doing it was the furthest thing from my mind. English and grammar had been by far my least favorite subjects in grade school, not so much for the content but for the timing of the classes. They always came right before lunch period, just as my blood sugar levels dropped and I lost my ability to concentrate. As the teacher droned on endlessly about sentence structure, gerunds, and adverbs the only thing I loved hearing about was onomatopoeia because the word sounded so cool as it rolled off her tongue. (Or, maybe because I was so hungry, I just liked the sizzling steak example she offered to illustrate the point.) I couldn't wait to rush home, gobble down lunch and return to the street to play ball with my friends.

Since I first sat down to start the book several seasons have passed and a very odd presidential election has come and gone. I have experienced successive bouts of thinking the work is pretty good to wondering why anyone would even want to read it. I thought it would be a linear process but after writing the beginning I have been skipping about, formulating the end and just pursuing thoughts as they come along. I'm not sure if this is how the creative process works or if I'm a closet dyslexic.

The project has been the source of both exciting moments and periods of absolute boredom. The work progresses in a series of ebbs and flows, starts and finishes. Some days I only accomplish a few poorly crafted paragraphs. But on other days the words just seem to flow as freely and forcefully as diarrhea from a Canadian goose. (Which I hope is more of a creative use of imagery rather than a comment on the quality of my writing.)

When you think about it, the written word is really an interesting concept. Although we tend to take it for granted, it's kind of amazing that a series of symbols on a piece of paper or computer screen can create precise images, deep thoughts, and hard-felt emotions. I have had a number of magazine articles published but am by no means a "natural born" writer. In fact, I find the task of writing to be a painful process. To me being a natural born writer is analogous to being a natural born killer: having the ability to do something that most people would find revolting.

My wife has published a number of novels and has the capacity to sit and write for hours. When I write I quickly get to the point where I want to stop and do something *real.* Finishing some carpentry work, going for a walk, or just staring out the window all provide comfortable escapes from the marathon effort of writing.

Inspiration has come when I wasn't even thinking about the task, like when I'm working out on my exercise bike or watching a movie. I have experienced the middle of the night "ah ha!" moments when I would furiously scribble on a notepad about some insight that was so enlightening and just had to be written down only to wake the next morning and discover that my undecipherable scratching revealed little more than my insomnia. (Thirty-three years in the firehouse have both destroyed my sleep patterns and deepened my appreciation for good Italian food.)

I believe that if there is any sort of writing muse it is probably more related to our body's natural biorhythms than any inspirational Greek spirit. Coffee, tea, or a nice piece of chocolate all seem to stimulate the creative juices. As does the enhancing beat of the Ramones or ZZ Top (but certainly not the soul-searching dirge of Pink Floyd or the sad introspection of Janis Ian). Some like to write in a library but when I'm in a public place I find myself staring at other people wondering if they might be involved in some task that is both easier and more enjoyable (also, you can't eat in the library and writing makes me hungry). I seldom accomplish two good writing days in a row and know I'm in trouble when I continually hit "word count" to see how many I've actually produced.

I also find myself striving for a colorful narrative while avoiding excessively colorful prose. Colors associated with writing have seldom been complementary. Noir, purple prose, and yellow journalism are not in my game plan. And while parts of my story are sad I don't want to leave the reader feeling blue. I remind myself that it is best to keep it black and white, basic and accurate. Some editor will undoubtedly slash many of my multihued descriptions prior to giving the green light to my efforts.

I actually did a lot of writing in my job. Just like any large government agency the FDNY generates reams of reports, personnel records, and training documents. Much of this material tends to be very factual and data driven. The task of producing it can feel like, as the humorist Jean Shepherd labeled it, writing with a chisel.

When I reached the rank of chief a substantial part of each tour was taken up in the process of sifting through piles of memos and correspondence. Some of it pertained to important issues about firefighting procedures, safety, and training. But much of it related to routine administrative matters. I always felt that things like overtime hours and vacation leave balances could have been handled more efficiently (and much more cheaply) by some civilian employee comfortably sitting in a headquarters cubicle. But ours was a unionized job and the last thing any union wants is to limit its members' job responsibilities and face the subsequent budget cuts that inevitably lead to fewer job openings and lower union membership.

Official fire department correspondence was prepared through a formal, structured process that reinforced my lack of interest in ever becoming a lawyer. I often felt constrained by the rigidity it demanded and struggled to crank out my message in the mandated style. The heading would always contain the requisite "To, From, Subject, Date" listing with perhaps an occasional "Via" added to complete the bureaucratic ambiance. At the bottom of the report you would enter "Respectfully Submitted" and sign your name, rank, and unit number regardless of whether you had in fact any respect at all for the recipient of the memo. (Though I must say that, with just a few exceptions, I did like and respect the people who were above me in the organization's pecking order.)

After a few years I got a lot more proficient in the art of producing such paperwork. My memos were often resplendent with the numerous abbreviations, mnemonic devices, and acronyms typical of any large organization. My reports became full of official words like "forthwith" and were lightly sprinkled with "viz" and other quasi-words.

But I never even approached the skills displayed by the classic authors of FDNY literature. That elite group had the ability to identify each subparagraph in the body of their reports with precise, Dewey decimal system–like labels (as in Section 2.3, Subsection 4a). To this day I am uncertain if my inability to do likewise stemmed from a mental failing on my part or from a fear of morphing into some kind of civil service zealot and carrying over such obsessive labeling to my supermarket shopping lists. Imagine, if you will, a section number 1 for dairy, a section number 2 for meats and fish, and subsections 1.1a and 1.1b for yogurt and cheese. Where, exactly, would one list tampons?

Regardless of the style or content all fire department correspondence was expected to religiously adhere to the chain of command. A company lieutenant preparing a report would have it first endorsed by the unit commander who in turn would forward it to the assigned battalion chief for review and then it would pass on to the deputy chief for his signature. The deputy chief would then send the report to the borough commander who would attach a comment and finally forward it to the agency head it was originally addressed to. Violations of the chain were few and far in between.

However, I did once see a break in the chain. One of my company commanders had some safety concerns and sent a memo directly to one of the agency heads without the usual intermediate endorsements. In the very first sentence of his letter he apologized for bypassing the normal process and explained that he just wanted to make some recommendations through an informal memo rather than an official report. His actions upset a lot of people and resulted in a flurry of subsequent official, chain-adhering correspondence. The company commander was eventually "admonished and instructed," as they say in department parlance, and reeducated on the sanctity of the bureaucratic process. Apparently procedure trumps initiative. Needless to say, I don't recall him ever again taking the time to come up with any other safety ideas.

Despite such tight control of our correspondence there were times when the wrong message was sent because of outright error or unintended suggestion. I once prepared a report on heart attacks since they are the cause of half of the firefighter deaths that occur each year. I thought it was pretty well written and was pleased to see that it was distributed to all of the fire units throughout the city—that is, until a friend called me from Brooklyn and pointed out that I had titled my report "The Treat of a Heart Attack" rather than "The Threat of a Heart Attack." Microsoft spellcheck had worked; my own editing had not. And one of our commissioners once sent out an official communication informing all that as of January 1 there would be zero tolerance for any alcohol consumption on the job (a position I was very much in agreement with). The only problem was that his edict was dated sometime in mid–December and left one wondering if it could be construed as some kind of tacit encouragement for squeezing in one last Budweiser-fueled romp before the year was over.

However, it must be said that the FDNY is not alone in occasionally failing to spot all the nuances of the written word. Recently, while driving home from a family vacation, I passed a topless joint that had a huge SALAD BAR sign plastered over the front windows. Were they suggesting that the clientele would be more impressed by the freshness of the croutons than the eroticism of the dancers? And consider, if you will, the obituary for William Burroughs that appeared in the *New York Times*. In one of the opening lines it nonchalantly reports that "he lived simply with three cats and indulged his interests in painting and photography and in collecting and discharging firearms," only to knock you over in a subsequent paragraph with the fact that he accidentally shot and killed his wife while enjoying one of his pastimes. I guess that good writing is akin to good comedy. Timing is everything.

Mindful of such pitfalls I continue with the challenge of writing the book though sometimes I wonder who exactly I'm writing for. Is it for some literary agent who will rapidly dismiss it as amateurish drivel? Or maybe it's for my kids who may someday stumble upon a dusty jumble of self-published words when they clean out the garage. Perhaps it's all just for myself to satisfy the timeless human need to say, "I was here. This is what I saw. This is what I thought." Had Hemmingway ever entertained such thoughts in between bouts of drinking and deep-sea fishing?

Writing is indeed a lonely process. When I was a firefighter I always had people around me. Now I find myself missing the rich cavalcade of sharp wit, high-volume humor, and unbridled flatulence that my former coworkers so cheerfully provided. Nevertheless, I return to the keyboard and fortified by my mantra ("250 poorly written words are better than no words at all, 250 poorly written words are better than no words at all..."), I continue onward.

And the torture begins again.

A Midnight Clear

I always liked the firefighting aspect of my job but viewed the administrative responsibilities as a necessary chore that just had to be done. Some of those responsibilities were really important but none of them had the pop and sizzle of managing a fire operation. That being said, one of the more significant administrative duties involved vacating buildings. As a deputy chief I was often called out to determine when a building had to have its occupants removed because of an existing fire danger or some potential structural hazard. In a city the size of New York this was a pretty routine task and a day seldom went by without some occupancy being vacated.

Performing this job gave me a front row view of the amazing variety of hovels that people had eked out for themselves in their effort to live in a city that was occasionally freezing and always expensive. It was not uncommon to discover a dozen men sleeping on mattresses in the basement of a closed store in the middle of the night with heavy, locked steel gates covering the entrance doors. The poor illegal immigrants who lived like this were more thankful for their warm, "secure" resting places than they were fearful of being trapped in a building with no way to get out.

I once observed a shanty town built of cardboard and scrap lumber cramped beneath the overpass of a busy Bronx highway. There were wires stretched to nearby streetlamps to power lights and televisions inside the tiny sheds. It looked more like something you would expect to see in a Brazilian slum than in the midst of the world's most vibrant city. But perhaps the most unlikely scenario was the discovery of a homeless man's mattress deep in the bowels of Penn Station. His home was just a few paces removed from the railroad tracks that countless commuters rode on every day. Buried beneath its glitter and wealth New York City definitely had its underside.

Not all of the building vacates involved places that people lived in. Theaters were a key part of New York culture but occasionally they also had safety issues. I nearly had to stop a Neil Young concert due to some serious concerns about the exit passages of the building he was scheduled to perform in. As it turned out the problem was rectified and the show wasn't canceled but delayed for about three hours. Fortunately, given the age and make-up of the audience, an ample supply of marijuana along with adequate bathroom facilities for prostate-enlarged men kept them patient and sedated despite the long delay. I couldn't stay to watch the performance but thought it would be kind of ironic if old Neil chose to sing his song about lying in a burnt-out basement.

Although I knew that I was performing an important and necessary task, I always felt somewhat like a villain when I had to force people out of a building, particularly if it was a residence. The occupants were re-located to places that were safer to live in but they also experienced an intense disruption of their lives. Imagine being told that you had three hours to gather your most important possessions before you had to leave your home with the possibility of not being able to come back until the required safety repairs were made. And that could mean for several weeks, or forever.

These traumatic removals could occur at any hour of the day on any day of the week. Holidays, including Christmas, were no exception. Christmas Eve is of course a special night for many people, regardless of their religious beliefs. The excitement and anticipation of childhood memories combined with the adult joy of observing your own children's delight sets it apart from other nights. As much as we all loved the fun and camaraderie of our job, none of us really wanted to work on Christ-mas. But the FDNY, like any other fire department, was a 24-hour op-eration and sometimes it was just your turn to work a holiday tour. It seemed like a special bonding occurred when you worked on Christmas. After a fire you would hear warm "Merry Christmases" exchanged be-tween the men as they packed the hose away and eagerly anticipated returning to the firehouse kitchen for the interrupted holiday meal that sat on the table.

One Christmas Eve I was sent to the Washington Heights section of Manhattan for a possible vacate in an apartment building. If you take a look at a map of the city you will see that Washington Heights is located in the northernmost section of Manhattan where the borough comes to a point and narrows down substantially. Alexander Hamilton once lived nearby and if he were still there today he'd be about a 20-minute subway ride to a mid–Manhattan theatre where he could watch himself being por-trayed by a frantically rapping actor (a performance that would no doubt leave him in a state of jaw-dropping confusion). The area is, and always was, considerably removed from what most people think of when they envision Manhattan. This too was Manhattan but the ass end of the borough, far removed from the midtown glitter and Wall Street money.

An elevated subway, the "El," was the spinal cord of Washington Heights, running straight through the middle of the neighborhood and transporting residents to the magical areas to the south or to the gray confines of the Bronx which sat just north on the other side of the Harlem River. The El had a timeless quality to it. The train cars were modern, silver conveyances that were largely devoid of the graffiti assaults of the 1970s. But the steel structure that supported the tracks was no different than the one you might watch in a grainy black and white movie from 1905.

The El was both a visual and acoustic assault on the people who lived near it. The huge steel pillars always blocked the sun from the shady sidewalks below and the steady flow of passing trains periodically shook the adjoining apartments to their very core. As in any locale the geography dictated the status, and rental costs, of the various sections of the neighborhood. There were expensive apartment buildings on the very fringe of the area with gorgeous views of the Hudson River. But as you moved away from that enclave the character of the environment changed radically. Generally, the closer you lived to the ancient, creaking El the lower your income level and the more desperate your life.

The vacate scenario I was called to on that Christmas Eve was located well within the desperate zone. The building was just like many that were crammed into the neighborhood. It was a large structure, five stories high with four or five apartments on each floor and narrow alleyways that barely separated it from the identical buildings right next door. The faded red brick walls and ancient fire escapes were typical of the area. Unfortunately it was also the type of place that sometimes housed a dwelling unit that was not in compliance with the city's fire codes and safety regulations. In the constantly slanted balance of supply and demand there were not always enough legitimate apartments available to provide the housing demands of the area's many residents. But there were always enough rent-hungry landlords who were willing to offer them rooms to live in whether they were legal occupancies or not.

The building may have been typical but the apartment in question certainly wasn't. All of the legal dwelling units were accessible by going through the front entrance door and walking up several flights of stairs. In the event of a fire those stairs would serve as the quickest and easiest way for residents to leave the building and a vital part of the firefighting strategy was dedicated to preserving that means of egress. If the stairs were blocked by smoke or fire the tenants could use the fire escapes as an alternate escape route.

However, the apartment I had been called to investigate was completely out of that safety zone. You could not get to it at all if you went through the front entrance. Instead, you had to go through a metal gate on the side of the building and walk about 40 feet down a narrow alleyway until you reached an area where the alley widened into a small courtyard. Like most longtime New York residents I had developed an ingrained "front door" perspective of the city and its buildings. That was the door I had used thousands of times in the apartment house in Brooklyn where I grew up. And that was the entrance I was trained to preserve as a firefighter. Most people in this city did not move through side alleyways. They entered a building through the front, an area that was familiar and comfortable and usually well-lit and often featured a front "stoop" which served as both a welcoming beacon as well as a sort of an urban social gathering place.

The courtyard I found myself standing in was none of those things. It felt confining and unwelcoming and was shadowed by the drab buildings that surrounded it. The alleyway that led to the courtyard was like a dark canyon surrounded by high brick walls that towered over it on both sides. Garbage cans were scattered about and you could almost sense the pres-

The traditional New York City stoop. This is how most, but not all residents, enter their homes (photograph by the author).

ence of the rats that no doubt fed from them. The passageway felt quite distant from the street and the rest of the building. In fact, it all seemed strangely removed from the city, as though it was Christmas Eve in a London slum in the 1840s rather than a scene in 21st-century New York. And this was the route that the occupants of this apartment followed each day as they went to and from their home.

You could enter through a heavily secured metal door that led directly to the courtyard. After the tenants let me inside I passed through a series of cramped, connecting rooms that were not vastly different from most of the other tenements I had seen, including the place where I had grown up. The furniture, clothing and photographs that were in each room gave evidence to the familial world that existed here. There was life in these rooms, a sense of comfort and warmth that contrasted sharply with the cold, indifferent courtyard that sat just on the other side of the old, battered entrance door. Unfortunately, there was also sickness here, as I quickly ascertained from the Hispanic family members who shared the apartment. An older woman was present, a grandmother, and she was quite sick with cancer.

The key element in determining whether an occupancy had to be vacated was to clearly establish the severity of any potential dangers. There were many apartments in New York that were not entirely legal but which could still provide a safe living space for people. That kind of situation was referred to the city's buildings department for investigation into compliance with the certificate of occupancy for the premises. The scenarios that I had to immediately act on were those that created living conditions that were "imminently" dangerous to life. You could never just walk away from locked or blocked exits, dangerous electric wiring, overcrowding or anything that might be construed as a threat to residents' lives. So far in my walk through the apartment I had seen none of those things. It wasn't until my firefighters pointed out the condition of the rear windows that I knew we had a serious issue on our hands. All were covered by secure metal bars, a common problem in any neighborhood where crime and security were a concern.

The danger was immediately obvious. The very same window bars that provided the family with a sense of security from a break-in could also kill them in case of a fire. The only way they could get out of their apartment was through their entrance door, if they could reach it through the smoke and flames. There was no room for any subtle interpretation of the law here; it doesn't get much more imminently dangerous than not having a second means of egress.

There were often times when I had to make difficult decisions at a fire and occasional times when I faced uncomfortable choices away from the fireground. This was one of those times. This was a very dangerous condition, one that couldn't be ignored, even on Christmas, even with a very sick person living in the apartment. On the other hand, it *was* Christmas and how do you order a family with a woman who may well be dying to leave their home? Even Ebenezer Scrooge cut Bob Cratchit some slack on that holiday and I didn't want Jacob Marley someday dragging his chains through my bedroom reminding me of my insensitivity.

I couldn't change the law but, for the safety of the family who lived here, I wanted to comply with it. So I decided to eliminate the problem. I ordered my men to cut the bars from the windows and they went right to work with their forcible entry tools. Normally they destroyed locks and steel bars to allow people to get out of a burning building. Now they were doing it to allow them to stay inside. Within minutes all the window bars were removed and the family had that vital alternate way out of the apartment that they would need if there was a fire.

Strictly speaking I was not allowed to do this. The fire department's job was to uncover hazardous conditions and to remove the residents when necessary. We were not in the business of rectifying these situations and I probably had no legal right to order my men to cut the window bars. But I have always been suspicious of anyone who clings to some esoteric passages of a rule book to determine how everything in life should work. There is as much to be said for enforcing the spirit of the law as there is for the letter of the law.

The rest of that night tour passed by pretty quietly and the next morning I was able to go home to my nice house and healthy family. That family in Washington Heights still had illness to deal with but at least they could deal with it in the familiar confines of their own apartment. I suspect that the grandmother is no longer still alive. But at least we were able to give her one more Christmas Eve in the comfort of her own home. We were able to take care of business. And to quote old Jacob Marley, "Business! Mankind *was* my business."

And Now,
Live on Scene...

Once I became a chief my duties on the fireground changed significantly. I became the eyes and ears of an operation, the guy who had to stay calm and objective and make the big strategic decisions on how we would fight the fire. At the same time I often became the voice of the operation, the one who would face the cameras and microphones and provide the sound and video bites for the evening news. In bureaucratese it was referred to as "interfacing" with the media and I had received no training on what to expect or how to handle it. So I was somewhat unprepared when I began to explore the art of looking like a professional, speaking without saying much, and politely resisting the media's best efforts at creating headlines that were not always accurate.

My exposure to interfacing was limited to what I had seen on television when a cop or a fire chief was interviewed. It seemed like they made ample use of words like "alleged," "perpetuator," and "forthwith," often in a heavily accented New York dialect. My own public speaking resume at that point was limited to a few mumbled lines in a grade school play and some rambling speeches I gave in high school or college. I had no noticeable accent and a fairly good vocabulary going in my favor but I still felt like a public information virgin suddenly thrown into the world of big-time New York City news media.

So with visions of performing like the next Water Cronkite or Anderson Cooper, I began to engage the on-scene reporters who came to my fires. The rapid transition from managing an intense and chaotic emergency scene to performing as a calm and informative representative of the FDNY took some effort. Kind of like what a boxer might feel when interviewed in front of a camera right after winning in a sixth-round knockout. I was able to watch quite a few of my television interviews on the five o'clock news within hours of a fire and would critique my media

150

performance in the same way that I would analyze the fire strategy and tactics we used. Had I come across sounding sufficiently official without relying too much on bureaucratic words like "incident," or "situation," or "deployment"? Did I remember to wear my hat or helmet to cover my hair which was generally so messed up after a fire that I looked like I had been wrestling with a bear?

I quickly learned the basics. Look at the reporter, the camera doesn't exist. Project with confident but approachable body language. Speak clearly and slowly and avoid overly technical words. And most important of all, don't say anything quotable or controversial if the incident involved a fatality or if there were any legal issues involved, a skill I was able to develop rather quickly having watched a lot of White House press secretaries in action. As Shakespeare would have put it, "He speaks yet says naught"—something I got better and better at doing.

Gradually it dawned on me that, whatever I said, it was going to be limited to a half-minute segment of a news broadcast and with verbal stumbling on my part edited out. And on a busy news day all the reporters really needed was a good camera shot of a burnt building and some brief, innocuous comments so they could move on to their next story. My confidence, and occasionally my cynicism, grew with each experience and I quickly learned about the show biz aspect of the news media. While each "award-winning" network was seeking the truth, or at least their version of the truth, they were also involved in an on-going ratings war.

This became apparent at a fire in a Manhattan apartment building one bitterly cold afternoon. An elderly woman had died in the fire and since the news channels monitored the fire department radio frequency a number of reporters showed up to the scene. A fatality always called for an investigation into the cause of the fire, a very detailed process involving considerable time and effort on the part of the fire marshals. Naturally, no pronouncement could be made until that investigation was complete or the case could be compromised in any subsequent legal proceedings.

When the fire was under control a reporter form one of the major news networks approached me for an interview. Our conversation went something like this:

REPORTER: Chief, can you tell us what started the fire?
ME: We don't have that information right now; the investigation is underway at this time.
REPORTER: Chief, is it possible that an electric space heater may have caused the fire?
ME: Our fire marshals will perform a thorough investigation, and I'd rather not speculate until they have sifted through the evidence.
REPORTER: Can you tell us if there was a space heater in the apartment?

ME: I don't have any information regarding that. We'll have to complete the
investigation to determine the facts.

After a few minutes of this it didn't take a rocket scientist to figure out
that this guy was looking for a story that would be a good fit for a newscast
on a frigid winter day. And, sure enough, when I turned on the 6 o'clock
news that evening his lead story was about the dangers of electric space
heaters.

Most of the reporters I met were polite and easy to work with. The
really aggressive ones were generally the exception but when they were at
the scene they seemed to stand out, and not always in a positive way. I had
a fire late one night in a Bronx apartment house and sadly a child had died.
While we were awaiting the arrival of the fire investigators I examined
the fire apartment to gather the dreary facts that were required for my
fatal fire report. Things like who had found the child, the exact position of
the body, possible causes for the fire, all the impersonal information that
had to be obtained before any evidence was compromised. It was never
a pleasant task and was especially trying when the victim was a little kid.
The dead child was still lying on the bed and my men were overhauling
the room to check for hidden pockets of fire when someone mentioned
to me that a reporter was in the street conducting an interview. Given all
the unanswered questions about the tragedy, I wondered who exactly she
might be talking to.

It turned out she had located the teenaged brother of the dead child
and was interviewing him before any official at the scene had an opportunity to speak with him. The reporter was a well-known veteran from a
major network who had been on television for years. She was really good
at what she did but, given the realities of a profession that emphasized
youth and photogenic assets, she had been relegated to on-scene work in
the field and replaced in the studio by a younger news anchor. And apparently she had used her skills and experience to jump on the possibility of
getting a news scoop about the fire. However, what none of us were aware
of at that moment was that the fire had been intentionally set by the very
teenager she was interviewing. I'm not sure if he even knew at that point
that his sister had died. I knew that the reporter was only doing her job
but to me the whole affair was a sad example of how sometimes that job
went beyond the scope of good journalism. I gave her the required on-air
interview a bit later but I did it with a chip on my shoulder. And I still think
of the incident whenever I happen to catch her on TV.

After a while the novelty of being interviewed on television or being
quoted in a newspaper article wore off and my involvement with the media
became a routine part of the job. However, one experience still stands out.

Just before New Year's Eve I responded to an incident on West 42nd Street near Times Square. Times Square was both the centerpiece of Manhattan and, from a media perspective, the center of the universe so the scene attracted hordes of reporters. About one half of an old six-story theatre had collapsed into the street just before rush hour and created the kind of havoc you'd expect in midtown. Bricks and rubble were strewn about tying up traffic and nearby subways were shut down. The situation was further complicated by the fact that it was less than 24 hours until the big Times Square New Year's Eve celebration. The event was set to mark the 100th anniversary of the consolidation of all five boroughs into what became greater New York. Part of the planned festivities involved giving out 30,000 balloons to the New Year's Eve revelers—balloons that had been stored in the collapsed theatre.

Building collapses call for slow and methodical work. It is not uncommon for these operations to go on for several days and initially it didn't seem likely the balloons would be available for New Years. However, it was quickly determined that the remaining sections of the building were stable enough to allow us to search for trapped victims. Thankfully there were none. When we had completed our search of the building the production coordinator of the New Year's Eve event approached me to see if the boxes of balloons that were stored inside could be safely removed. Since there was no danger of further collapse I allowed my men to drag several boxes of them out to the sidewalk. I gave no further thought to the balloons and forgot all about them once I left the scene.

However, the event producer certainly had not forgotten. She was interviewed by the *New York Times* and next morning's paper had a long article about the collapse and the department's involvement in saving the balloons. In the article she thanked me personally and called me the "savior" of the New Year's balloons. I felt uncomfortable with being labeled as the savior of anything since it was the firefighters who had done all the work. Nonetheless, there I was, in black and white, right on the bottom of page B4 of the *New York* Friggin' *Times*. I had made the grade. I had been judged worthy to be included in "All the News That's Fit to Print" and achieved that 15 minutes of fame that Andy Warhol had promised to all. And yes, I still keep an old, yellowed clipping of my "savior" article tucked away in an envelope, ready to be whipped out if I ever need to win the evangelical vote in a tight election.

The extent of media coverage at an incident usually depended on which borough you were working in. When just about anything happened in mid–Manhattan you could expect the major national networks to be there in an instant. Once you got into the outer sections of the city our work just wasn't given the same coverage unless something really unusual occurred like a fire with multiple causalities or a plane crash. Out in the boroughs the reporters who covered our fires generally worked for the local cable news station which was sort of a version of television's minor leagues. They contrasted sharply with the broadcasters from the well-financed news machines of NBC, CBS, and ABC who tended to be older and more experienced and were backed by large communications vans laden with enormous antennas that looked like they could transmit signals to Mars.

On the other hand, the "small guy" from the local station was usually a young woman who looked like she was six months removed from her bachelor's degree in communications. She would arrive at the scene in a sub-compact car that had the station's logo on the door and her only "back up" was a guy who carried both the small handheld camera and micro-phone that made up the extent of their technical resources.

I always tended to favor the small cable station reporters. I felt that if I gave them a good interview I could somehow help them along on their career paths to bigger and better jobs. Their neat business attire and perky young smiles stood out in sharp contrast to the drab beats they were as-signed to cover. I would often look at them and imagine what my own young daughter would be like in just a few years.

I did see some similarities between the tasks the media performed and the work that we did. We both had difficult jobs that involved racing to disasters throughout the city in all kinds of weather at all hours of the day and night. And there was no predictable routine in either of our pro-fessions. Any quiet workday could suddenly be interrupted by an incident with enormous consequences that required an immediate size-up, evalu-ation, and gathering of vital information.

However, there were also some major differences between our two worlds. For one thing, no matter what kind of challenge we faced in the fire department we were all on the same page, using the same procedures, and working together to resolve the problems. On the other hand, the various news outlets often seemed to be vying with each other, trying to scoop exclusive stories, make deadlines, and advance in the on-going ratings war. Their world was competitive; ours was more of a close-knit community. And of course, when you come right down to it the reality that always separated us from most other professions was the unspoken possibility of injury or death that was always present on the fireground. Still, it was kind of exciting to be a part of the news even though the kind of news we tended to generate was seldom pleasant stuff.

The Day After

Before I joined the FDNY I never fully understood why there were beds in a firehouse. When I visited my father's firehouse as a child I found the very idea of having a place to sleep while you were at "work" to be kind of odd if not outright indulgent. All the other dads from my neighborhood traveled to their nine-to-five jobs each morning and eight or nine hours later they returned home looking somewhat fatigued but ready for the evening's activities. None of them slept on their jobs (at least as far as I and their employers were aware of). They climbed into their beds around the same time every night and caught up with their unfinished chores on the weekends. In contrast my father sometimes fell sound asleep in the middle of the afternoon while he sat on the couch reading the newspaper. I would look at him and wonder how he could be so tired. It was the daytime and the entire world was outside pursuing activities and accomplishing tasks. It was as if everyone else was on a different timetable.

As I got older most of my friends took the train to Manhattan for their jobs but they too came home each evening eager to shoot some eight ball at the local pool hall or to toss the football around in the street. Commuter fatigue might set in by Thursday but that was easily overcome with a good night's sleep or a relaxing weekend.

I didn't know any firefighters other than my father nor did I really understand what their work world was like. Most of the men from the neighborhood had "normal" jobs with predictable hours and stable routines. I'm sure they got coffee breaks but the ones who worked in factories had no mattresses to fall into and the Wall Street clerks could not curl up in a comfy blanket. They weren't exactly going to stumble upon a plush futon sitting right next to the lathe or the copying machine. If you told them there was a job that provided beds to rest in they probably would have assumed that it was some kind of a no-show position created by a union mob boss.

I had that same perspective when, as a nine-year-old, I first saw the bunkroom of Engine Company 215, where my father worked. That particular unit was disbanded decades ago during one of New York City's fiscal crunches but the images are still very clear in my mind. The company was housed in an ancient, three-story building and had the high tin ceilings, coal storage bins, and intricate masonry work that gave those old firehouses such soul. The bunkroom was a large, undivided room located on the second floor. The windows always seemed to be covered by dark green shades that gave the space an inviting, dimmed ambience even in the middle of the day. And in an era before air conditioning became common, each of the bunks was covered by finely meshed mosquito nets, a feature which seemed very exotic and made it look more like a 19th-century malaria ward than a 20th-century firehouse. All in all it looked like a very inviting place to rest, nice and dark and very old-fashioned, kind of like what it would be like to take a nap inside a museum.

As appealing as the bunkroom was, it still didn't answer the question of why it existed or explain the strange intermixing of sleep time and work time. Those answers would become abundantly obvious years later when the firehouse world also became my work world. For most of my time on the job I worked 24-hour shifts. The upside to that schedule was that I only commuted to work eight times a month. To people who are used to a daily, grinding nine-to-five routine the concept of going to work just twice a week might sound very appealing. But there was a big difference between a nine-hour and 24-hour work period. I always tended to work in active fire units where I was guaranteed to respond to a lot of emergency calls at all hours of the day and night. Even on the rare quiet night I was often assigned to house watch duties which meant staying up most of the night answering phone calls and acknowledging the alarms when they were sent in by the dispatcher. In addition, until I was promoted to chief I was also required to work a lot of additional overtime tours and that meant that I would have to be on duty on what would have normally been my day off. Often it seemed like an endless cycle of recuperating from exhaustion, followed by more exhaustion.

I usually found that the physical work of being a firefighter combined with the round-the-clock responses and occasional nocturnal administrative duties exhausted me to a point where I could just collapse into my bunk and slip into a nap, often to be suddenly awakened by yet another emergency response. Whatever sleep I did manage to get was very sporadic and constantly interrupted. It was more like periodically passing out rather than truly going to sleep. Friends of mine who were not firefighters just didn't seem to get this. They were amazed that I could be so tired after working a 24-hour tour in a firehouse that had beds to sleep in. I couldn't quite explain to them that most often I got to lie down for just an hour or two, if even that much. Some of these friends also thought that I was always at home because when they would call me from their office jobs on a Wednesday afternoon I was there to answer the phone while they were working. They assumed that I was living a life of ease, an attitude I found rather frustrating and I felt like telling them to try calling me on a Saturday night or on Thanksgiving or Christmas when I would be working and they were enjoying themselves like the rest of the normal world.

For all of the many positive things I got out of my work it also had the downside of putting me out of sync with any semblance of a circadian rhythm and it alienated me from the normal social routines of life. I finally understood that image of my father falling asleep on the couch. He was just feeling what I felt, what every firefighter felt, that utter weariness that inevitably came on the day after most of your work tours. Yes, there were beds in the firehouse but the demands of the job, as well as the realities of the bunkroom, did not lend themselves to allow for sufficient rest while you were at work. In fact, my actual adult experience of being in the firehouse bunkroom could not have been more different from the brief glimpse of it that I had as a child. It was less like sleeping in a museum and much more like sleeping in the focs'l of a pirate ship.

The firehouse bunkroom, like the crew's quarters on an old sailing ship, was basically a room which contained a lot of beds all carefully aligned to fit a large group of men into a small space. If you were the type who craved privacy you were definitely in the wrong place. For with that large group of men also came inevitable bouts of competitive snoring which were occasionally interrupted by hearty expressions of freelance flatulence. The evening "sleep" time ran from approximately 11 p.m. to about 7 a.m. but was not really one continuous period. Instead it was a long series of abrupt starts and finishes as the men were suddenly awakened for emergency responses. Kind of like the "All hands on deck!" call to the crew of a ship being battered by a storm only the firehouse responses were announced by large, bright fluorescent ceiling lights that were suddenly turned on to shock anyone who had fallen into a dream state followed by the ringing of loud bells which shook the very souls of those few who were not jolted awake by the lights. One South Bronx firehouse I worked in even had a deafening klaxon horn that blasted when a run came in. It was an exact replica of the sound you hear in a movie when a U-boat dives and was piercing enough to wake the dead.

The alarms were transmitted from the dispatcher to a computer which was constantly manned by the house watchman and they were always preceded by an electronic "ding-dong" sound. I developed a Pavlovian response to this sound after hearing it for decades. Whether I was awake or asleep the tone would instantly create a surge of adrenaline which I guess prepared me to do the work I had to suddenly perform but at the same time beat the crap out of my body after hearing it at least 30 times over the course of a tour. To this day, and probably for the remainder of my days, I still get that same jolt of nervous energy and anticipation whenever I hear anything that approximates that tone. Sometimes I get brief painful flashbacks to that feeling when I press a neighbor's doorbell button. I can't even begin to explain my slightly dazed appearance when they come to the door.

You wouldn't find anyone working on a scrimshaw project in the bunkroom but, just as in the crew's quarters of a sailing ship, you would hear the occasional bitching and moaning. There was no talk of mutiny but there were snippets of conversation before guys passed out on their beds. Following the eighth or ninth run of the night the exhaustion would easily lead to comments about that dumb chief who had no idea what he was doing or complaints about the chauffeur of that nearby engine company who had the audacity to steal our hydrant at the last job.

Sometimes a relatively quiet tour might be disturbed when a guy who wasn't even working showed up in the middle of the night. Usually he was scheduled to work the following day and either wanted to avoid the morning rush hour or was seeking a comfortable resting spot following a night of carousing. You would hear him stumbling in and whether he was sober or buzzed his blind search for an available bed always added to the Grand Central Station ambiance of the bunkroom.

In the midst of all this activity there were some individuals who actually could sleep. They would be out the moment their heads hit the pillow and seemed oblivious to all that was going on around them. I would see them in the kitchen the following morning looking as fresh as a daisy, like they had spent the night in a relaxing hotel room. I hated those guys or at least I really envied the DNA or peace of mind or whatever it was they possessed that allowed them to sleep through an artillery barrage.

While I was sleep challenged as a firefighter I became absolutely sleep deprived when I moved up the ranks of the fire department. As a firefighter I basically had only myself to take care of. There was a mental aspect to the job but much of my activity was purely physical and all of the leadership, as well as the important fireground decisions, were the responsibility of the company officer. Even though I would be suddenly jolted awake I was thoroughly acquainted with the procedures and techniques I had to perform at a fire and was generally spared from the weight of having to make any vital strategic decisions. I was part of a team of firefighters that functioned well as a unit and didn't ask too much of any one individual.

That all changed once I became a company officer and it really got ramped up when I was a chief. Now I was the one who had to make instantaneous decisions at a fire that would not only affect the outcome of the operation but, even more crucially, determine the safety of the men I supervised. As a company officer I was responsible for five men. As a chief there were situations in which there might be 150 firefighters under my command. All it would take was one bad decision on my part to possibly place those men in positions of danger. While I felt capable of safely running an emergency operation the very thought of the responsibility I carried was always a concern that kept me somewhat on edge. I thought of that as being a good thing because in my line of work you never wanted to relax to a point where you were taking things for granted or getting too lax in your approach to the work.

Such concerns definitely affected my fatigue level as I rose in rank. While my sleep patterns as a firefighter were pretty awful they got much worse as a chief. I hated the feeling of being abruptly awakened in the middle of the night and suddenly thrust into a situation where I had to make life-and-death decisions in the stressful confines of the fireground. I much preferred to stay awake most of the night to avoid the shock of that experience. Sometimes I would catch up on some administrative work and then spend my nights reading a book, watching television, or just lying down and monitoring the department radio.

Listening to that radio kept me in touch with what was going on out in the field and, just as important, prepared me to spring into action in the event I had to instantly function as the incident commander of a serious fire. The radio traffic was endless and much of it was for standard emergencies or false alarms. After years of listening to that radio I could readily tell just from the voice intonations of the messages being broadcast whether yet another routine response or a major incident was about to unfold. You always knew when a good job was coming in. The dispatcher's voice would be terse and more serious as he would inform you that they were getting "numerous phone calls" or "reports of people trapped," information that would immediately get your heart beating. In minutes this would be followed by the "10–75" signal given by the officer of the first fire unit to arrive at the scene which announced that he had a working fire. You could tell much about that officer even if you didn't know him well. A new guy would tend to yell an excited "10–75!" as if to say, "Holy shit! We've got a fire!" as opposed to the more subdued "10–75" of a seasoned veteran who would also provide a brief description of the building involved.

After a while I kind of gave up on sleep and found that, with a few cups of coffee in me, I could function without it. If a fire came in near the end of my tour the adrenaline produced by that event would sharpen me right up even if I hadn't slept at all. The only time I would really hit the proverbial brick wall was when I had to produce some detailed administrative report after a particularly rough night. There were times when I actually nodded off at the keyboard of my office computer. I once read that the Army field manual requires that a terrorist detainee must be allowed at least four hours of sleep over a 24-hour period in order to be in compliance with the rules of the Geneva Convention. In theory if Osama bin Laden had been captured alive he would have gotten more sleep than I did on the job.

Needless to say, this all caught up with me on the day after. Just like my dad had been years ago I was a man totally out of sync. The eight days a month I went to work were always followed by two or three days off but, at least on that first day off, I was somewhat useless as a functioning person who was capable of making a totally rational decision about anything. It seemed like my mind would recoup at about the same rate as my body and I would use that first day to perform mindless chores like paying bills or food shopping. I would never even attempt to make any important decisions on that day and found that even my eating habits were affected. Sometimes supper seemed like an appealing meal at 10 a.m. followed by breakfast around 4 in the afternoon.

I was off on a lot of weekdays and one of the advantages of my schedule was that the stores were not as crowded as they would be on weekends when "normal" people shopped. The same was true of the parks that I enjoyed walking through which were usually empty except for groups of kids with their babysitters. Even there I would stick out because, other than the older retired guys, I was often the only man present and sometimes got suspicious looks from the Jamaican nannies as they carefully shielded the flocks of young children they cared for. I almost felt the need to explain that I was not a threat, just a tired guy hanging out on his day off.

In truth I guess that I *looked* suspicious, or at least unemployed, as I roamed about the fringes of the nine-to-five world trying to recapture some semblance of circadian normalcy. Sitting there in a Starbucks sipping coffee and reading my newspaper I was often surrounded by Spandex-clad women fresh from Pilates and would wonder just where all the men were. Of course, most of them were at work and dealing with their own routines.

I've been retired now for about two years. I no longer have any "days after" to slough my way through and I sleep according to a relatively normal timetable. While I miss the job I do not miss being abruptly awaked at 3 a.m. for a fire on a snowy, 20- degree night. Finally, after 33 years of an awkward life schedule, I am living more or less like everyone else. Gone are the days of extreme mental and physical exhaustion. They have been replaced by standard day-to-day moments of fatigue that stem from life's demands or low blood sugar levels. However, I still find myself waking up a few times in the middle of the night. Sometimes I just lie there for a while and think about the day's events. Other times I will grab one of the books I keep near my bed and read a bit. Then, whenever I feel ready, I casually roll over and ease my way back into the serenity and comfort of what I know will be an uninterrupted dream state. And to me that's a real luxury. For that is a place I seldom entered when I was in the firehouse.

We're Only Human

Recently, I picked up a book by Foster Huntington titled *The Burning House*. It raised an interesting question. The author surveyed people to determine what they would bring with them if they had to suddenly flee from their burning homes. The results showed an eclectic mix of things they would need or want, ranging from teddy bears to shotguns. Practical things like money, clothing, and laptops, along with jewelry and other valuables, all ranked high in importance. At the same time possessions that had no monetary value, or little practical need, such as stuffed animals and letters from friends, were also significant for a lot of people.

The survey reinforced the fact that humans are extremely complex creatures with diverse needs and priorities. What is essential for one individual may be completely irrelevant for someone else. Your choice of things to retrieve from that burning house reflects personal interests and priorities. One person may want their grandfather's World War II medals. Another, as illustrated in a story that appeared recently on the Internet, would actually go back into a burning home to get his beer. Personally speaking, I wouldn't want the beer but if I thought about it I could probably come up with an odd list of things that would be significant to me.

While the book focuses on the specific objects people value, it also leads to broader questions about how people may generally react to fires and other disasters. It is human nature to feel somewhat personally immune to many of the bad things that occur "out there." Hurricanes, earthquakes, and floods are often viewed from a distance on the Internet or television and are seen as events that happen to other people. Practically speaking, there is a beneficial aspect to this belief. If you really thought about all the potential disasters that always exist (terrorist activity, heart attack, robbery, etc.), you would probably have a difficult time just getting out of bed in the morning.

I got to see a lot of people in crisis situations over the course of my career. The fires, building collapses, and other disasters they encountered stripped them of their ordinary, day-to-day routines and mindsets. What was left was raw fear and their reactions to that fear. And while I did everything possible to safely manage those scenarios I also tried to learn things about human behavior when I observed their actions. Kind of like a fire chief/psychologist/sociologist, though you'd have a really hard time fitting that into a civil service job title.

One of the first things I noted was how strongly people would cling to their normal routines regardless of what might be going on around them. Panic was not the norm. If anything, the challenge was often to get them to act and overcome the lethargy that would often set in due to the genetic and social influences that arose in a moment of crisis. Disaster history is full of such examples. In 1977 there were 167 fatalities at the Beverly Hills Supper Club fire in Kentucky. There were a lot of factors involved but one major issue was the initial casual approach to the fire. There was a delayed notification to the fire department, a common thread of many fire deaths. The club employees were more inclined to follow their usual chain of command and tell their supervisors about a problem rather than taking initiative on their own. And the club patrons were just as nonchalant. One of them apparently ordered a rum and Coke to go in the early stages of the fire which, in retrospect, seems absurd but just reinforces the natural tendency we all have to deny or downplay potentially threatening situations.

We even saw elements of this behavior in the early stages of 9/11. As the North Tower was burning many of the occupants in the South Tower were, understandably, uncertain of what to do. Some of them were advised by security personnel to stay in their offices because they thought they would not be affected by what was going on outside. There were even instances of workers initially exiting to the street only to return to their desks and die when the second plane hit. Many of those who did choose to leave did not do so immediately. A survey of survivors indicated that a thousand of them took the time to shut down their computers before they left their desks. It would be unfair to say that their actions were wrong. They were just acting the way humans do. And I know exactly how they felt because if I suddenly smelled smoke as I write this line I would immediately investigate where it was coming from but I would probably also take a second to hit the "save" button and not lose my work.

The Beverly Hills Supper Club fire and 9/11 were massive, high-profile disasters that have been the subject of intense study and analysis. But I also saw examples of denial in many of my "normal" day-to-day fire operations. New York City is a very busy place, especially in the daytime. This was especially true of mid–Manhattan at rush hour. When I was a deputy chief I was usually positioned at a command post located in the street right in front of the building that was burning. I was amazed at how often we needed the police to cordon off my workspace to keep pedestrians away from the operation. It often seemed like in their frantic need to get to where they were going they were oblivious or indifferent to what was happening around them. I liked to refer to it as "Manhattan myopia." There were even instances when the firefighters took matters in their own hands when a hoard of people would mob their work area by having a brief "accidental" misdirection with the hose line. There's nothing like a wet suit to encourage crowd control.

However, I witnessed the preeminent example of people clinging to their normal routines at a job in the Bronx. We were operating at a gas leak in a large strip mall that contained about eight separate stores. The entire building was evacuated and the customers quickly left the scene and blended into the neighborhood. All except the bar patrons. They decided to set up chairs on the sidewalk right in front of the bar and continued tapping beer kegs like nothing unusual had happened. From the look of their pasty faces it seemed like they spent a substantial part of each day imbibing in the inner recesses of that dark tavern. They weren't going to allow the possibility of a major building explosion to distract them from their normal activity, even if it was 11 in the morning.

The great thing you see in most people is their tendency to bond and help each other when they are facing a disaster. Once they have evacuated their homes and grabbed those items they deemed necessary to take with them they are likely to behave very altruistically to their neighbors and even to strangers. I saw this in my own neighborhood during Hurricane Sandy. Trees were downed throughout the area, roads were impassible, and many of us were without electricity for two weeks. Over that period I got to see and interact with neighbors I seldom ran into. They all helped each other through the crisis and there was a sense of community you normally just didn't see. The exact same spirit was so obvious in New York City during the difficult weeks after 9/11.

Disaster brings people together. Well, most of the time. The exceptions are rare but when they do occur they really stick out in your memory. One such exception occurred in the Bronx. I was commanding a fire in one of the borough's nicer neighborhoods. It was a pretty good job with heavy fire venting out of two windows and thick, black smoke pushing out throughout the building. We were still in the process of stretching hose lines and searching for victims when the resident of the building next door approached me at my command post. He looked very upset and I thought he might have some important information about the occupants of the burning building so I gave him my immediate attention.

It turned out that some of the window glass and other debris from the fire had landed in his front yard, and though it wasn't burning or presenting any immediate danger to him or his building, he demanded that it be immediately removed from his property. Managing any fire in its early stages is a very intense and stressful experience that requires a good deal of concentration regardless of all the distractions. There's a lot going on and the rapid decisions you make will set the tone for the successful completion, and safety, of the operation. And this guy had the audacity to interrupt my train of thought for this? His next-door neighbor's house was burning and all he could think about was the temporary inconvenience it was causing him.

I had achieved a pretty high rank as a deputy chief in the FDNY and I always tried to conduct myself in a professional manner that showed the job in a positive light. So despite my anger, I told Mr. Empathy that we would take care of the debris as soon as we could. But somehow, after the story was retold a few times, the word got around that I had told the guy to go fuck himself. I certainly had not but I never corrected the rumor because it made a great story and the guys ate it up. And it's also what I would have liked to have said to him.

You could find the occasional callous person like him in any part of the city, but I usually observed people supporting each other when their buildings burned. However, I did notice that people's responses to fire varied according to the neighborhood they lived in. I don't know if anyone has ever done a sociological study comparing how residents react to a fire in the different boroughs but I certainly noticed a difference between mid–Manhattan and the Bronx. At the risk of sounding politically incorrect I'd have to say that Bronx residents were, overall, tougher people than those who lived in midtown. Bronx dwellers lived harder lives and saw a lot more fires. It was not uncommon for some of them to experience several fires in their apartment buildings over a relatively short time. It almost got to a point where a fire was kind of expected and was no big deal. I once stretched a hose line through a Bronx apartment because it had a window that allowed us to operate the nozzle on a fire in an adjoining building. The apartment itself was not at all affected by the fire but the couple who lived in it seemed completely indifferent to the fact that a bunch of guys were stomping around their home wrestling a hose line into position. They just continued watching television as oblivious to us as they would be to the guy who read the gas meter.

Mid–Manhattan residents were different. They lived in better surroundings and seldom experienced fires. When they did it was always a major event and they were often uncertain how to react. Many of them were foreigners or young people from other parts of the country and some didn't have a clue of how to survive in a high-rise building. They were always appreciative of our work but those who were new to the city were sometimes bewildered by how we worked. I once handled a minor stove fire in a midtown high-rise and the occupants thought they had to write us a check for coming to their home and extinguishing it. I found their naïve sincerity kind of appealing and, after joking that we only accepted VISA cards, I explained that we were in the business of making house calls and not charging for them.

Regardless of what borough a fire occurred in there was often a tendency toward "group think." I found that when people were facing a crisis they often debated and discussed among themselves what to do. The general sequence of their emotions progressed from denial to discussion and finally to a course of action. Sometimes it just took one person to step up and initiate a move and the rest of the group would follow. And that could be good or bad depending on what direction they decided on.

Group think mindset is just another general human characteristic and is not peculiar to any band of people. You will see the same behavior wherever you go. I was staying in a hotel in Virginia recently and the fire alarms went off throughout the building. Of course, it came at the worst possible time—when I was taking a shower. My son called the lobby and everyone was advised to leave the building. Now I've got this routine every time I check into a hotel. The very first thing I do is check to see if the television is working. Having established that, I go out into the hallway and check for the nearest emergency exit. It's kind of ingrained. And it never made a difference until this time. I knew that the closest exit was just down to the right of our room. Yet there was a crowd of people marching to the left for another exit that was considerably further away. Someone had initially gone in that direction and the group just followed along. I grabbed a towel, dried myself off, and my son and I left our room, made a quick right and went down the closest stairway to the street. It turned out to be just a false alarm but served as a good lesson for my son about being aware of your surroundings and thinking independently.

It remains to be seen how the experiences of 9/11, along with the constant paranoia about terrorism, might affect people's long-term behavior. There were some temporary, short-term reactions. Immediately after 9/11 many people moved out of New York City. Others were, understandably, afraid to fly and instead chose to drive to their destinations. Ironically, this led to an increase in automobile fatalities. There were also positive effects from the kinship that was experienced in the city immediately following the attack. As Sebastian Junger points out in his book *Tribe*, in the six months after 9/11 the murder rate in New York dropped by 40 percent and the suicide rate by 20 percent.

I was wrong about one thing. I had assumed that the harsh blast of real fear, chaos, and disaster that was streamed on live television on 9/11 would substantially change people's interests and perspectives. It seemed to make sense that such terror would give people a more realistic view of danger and make them shy away from "reality" dramas in the media. But you only have to look at cable television programing to realize that, for better or worse, we are what we are. And we still like to watch shows that portray people trying to survive in the wilderness (naked or clothed), fishing on dangerous crab boats, or driving trucks through the frozen Alaska wilderness. We may not seek out danger but we sure like to watch it.

I think it is safe to say that the human capacity for resilience, combined with our need to feel that things are "normal," is likely to keep our behavior in crisis situations similar to what it has always been. To some extent that behavior will be tempered by the background, personality, and training of the individual. Some will hold up better under stress, remain calmer, and make practical decisions. Others will not. As illustrated in *The Burning House*, there are those who will bring blankets and those who will bring lipstick.

What would you bring? Would your choice of items reflect your sentimental or practical side? Our choices are not always logical or predictable. That burning house represents more than property being destroyed. It also signifies a severe disruption of a person's memories, daily habits, and usual sense that disaster is something that only happens to other people.

The Papers

It's difficult to write about 9/11. What more can I possibly add to the volume of books, memoirs, and articles that have already been produced by those who experienced, and suffered, so much more than I? As overwhelming and tragic as the event was it is already starting to be viewed by many as a part of history. About one-fifth of the current American population was not even born on that day. And one-quarter were too young to have any real memories of the attack. Still, in many ways it is the defining moment for both the FDNY and New York City. The "where were you when" question no longer pertains to Pearl Harbor but to 9/11.

I was at work that day in the northern section of the city, which is a story in itself. I often think about the number of chance encounters and quirks of fate that, without any indication, radically change our lives. It was not foresight, courage, or intelligence that left me unscathed on 9/11. It was more like a simple roll of the dice.

Just a few weeks prior to the attack I was still assigned as a chief in mid–Manhattan. The area was fascinating to be in and I enjoyed the challenge of working in the middle of the country's biggest city. Unfortunately, the fire commissioner liked to frequently reassign personnel. This would normally be a good method of rounding out your experience and training. However, we were being moved about so often that it was difficult to get to really know your personnel and to learn the peculiarities of your response area. It was hard to feel settled at work since you never knew how long you could stay in one place. I was in the middle of a meeting with my battalion chiefs one July afternoon when I received a phone call from headquarters informing me that, effective immediately, I was being transferred to lower Manhattan.

I wasn't thrilled to be making yet another move but I was certainly not the only person involved. Dozens of other chiefs were also being transferred and, as things turned out, far more than their careers were to be affected. Some left work locations that probably would have killed them

168

had they stayed and others were moved to new assignments that lead to their deaths on 9/11.

Just prior to moving on to lower Manhattan I found out that there was an opening for a deputy chief in another section of the city. Division 7 covered half of the Bronx and the northern part of Manhattan. It didn't have the pizazz or high profile of the midtown world I had gotten used to and much of the area was rundown and poor. However, it was a very busy area with much more fire activity. For a few days I obsessed about the merits of taking the opportunity to move to the 7th Division as opposed to just following the original plan of going to lower Manhattan. As I often did when confronted with a difficult or conflicting decision I decided to go for a long walk in the woods. They say you should follow your gut and not overthink things. While I was on that walk my gut told me to take the assignment in the northern part of the city and within days I found myself in the Bronx.

I've often thought about this decision and how it affected my life and how lucky I have been. If I had just gone with the flow and dutifully reported to the original assignment in lower Manhattan would I have been at the site when the buildings came down? Would I have survived? Or, even more disturbing, had some other chief died in place of me? Surely one can get hopelessly lost in such conjecture and it's probably best not to go there.

It was pure circumstance that placed me on duty in the Bronx on that beautiful Tuesday morning and I have a memory shared by so many others of how crystal clear the sky was that day. I was listening to the morning news and starting to plan the day's work activities when I heard about what was assumed to be a small plane hitting one of the Trade Center towers. I immediately turned up the volume on both the TV and the fire department radio and, like countless others, watched what was unfolding.

I always found the act of being detached from a fire or emergency and observing it from a distance to be a frustrating and unnerving experience. Even if I was not at the scene I couldn't help but look at it from a "professional" perspective. What was happening? What needed to be accomplished and how could you best position the resources needed to resolve the problem? What were the prime safety considerations? And, of course, how well would I be able to perform if I was commanding this incident?

I watched the North Tower burn and thought about the strategy and tactics that would be needed. The firefighting problems were greatly amplified given the volume of fire and the number of people in the building. Still, I initially felt that the challenge would be handled by the resources of our department. It would certainly be a long and difficult battle but as I gazed at the TV screen I believed it was a battle that we would eventually win as we always had in the past. Then the unthinkable happened.

There are thousands of high-rise structures in New York City and the FDNY responds to hundreds of fires and emergencies in them each year. Years of experience in these buildings have refined the procedures and techniques to a point where a high-rise operation is often routinely handled despite the unique challenge it presents. Other than an occasional small, localized weakening of a concrete floor or ceiling the possibility of a major collapse occurring at a high-rise fire is not even a consideration. Containing the fire, determining the extent and location of the smoke condition, and a rapid search of stairways and public hallways are the immediate concerns. The only time I ever recall anyone even planning for a possible high-rise collapse was at a fire that occurred in Philadelphia in 1991 which killed three firefighters. That fire burned through eight floors of an office building over a 10-hour period until it was finally held in check by just 10 sprinkler heads on an upper floor.

When the North Tower collapsed I stared in disbelief at the TV screen. I was astounded that such an event was even possible and I was appalled by the unimaginable loss of life that had just occurred. More than a building had been destroyed. An entire sense of what constituted "normal" reality had been obliterated in a heartbeat.

For the next several hours I was in the strange position of both watching the horror as it unfolded and at the same time functioning in my capacity as an emergency response leader. My attention wavered between listening to the intense, live fireground radio transmissions from the scene and seeing the images on the television screen. The office phones were ringing constantly with questions and offers of assistance. Somehow an EMS unit in the state of Maine had gotten my number and offered to have their ambulances respond to New York City. Again, under "normal" conditions this would be an absurd offer but given the enormity of the situation I asked them to send down whatever they could spare. Sadly, there would turn out to be very little need for their help since there were many more dead victims than treatable patients.

Throughout all this I was constantly on the edge of my seat, expecting at any moment to be assigned to the Trade Center. At any one time there are nine deputy chiefs on duty in various sections of New York City. I knew that there would be at least three already at the scene. I didn't know that one was already dead. And as the phones, the radios, and the TV blared in the background I began to wrestle with both my fears and responsibilities. If I was dispatched down there what would it be like? I imagined a chaotic nightmare and wondered what kind of command structure would exist and tried to envision what steps I could possibly take to establish some semblance of control of a situation that nobody had ever faced before. What, if anything, was left of the FDNY bureaucracy and if I was sent to the scene would I be put in the position of having to make some impossible decisions?

All these thoughts were circling through my head when the second tower collapsed. It wasn't a shock the way the first one was. What had seemed impossible had happened once and in an absurd, horrific way it almost made sense that it would happen again. I imagined that 50,000 people had just been killed but couldn't even get a mental grip on the idea of so many deaths. I heard the Manhattan dispatcher broadcast a request for *any* fire unit at the scene to acknowledge and respond on their fireground radio—only to be met with absolute silence. And along with the horror and fear of it all was a sense that to this day is difficult for me to reconcile.

After the South Tower fell I was plagued by thoughts of what to do if I was sent down there and put in a position where I had to make some command decisions. And I came to the harsh conclusion that the only thing to do would be to order all of the firefighters out of the North Tower. Would I have ordered the abandonment of the largest rescue operation in the history of the United States? Yes, I would have. But at the same time I knew that it would be a choice that would haunt me for the rest of my life. It so much went against the grain of traditional, aggressive FDNY strategy. However, as I pondered all of this there was a very competent chief working in the lobby of the North Tower who had the courage to make that exact decision. Unfortunately, not all of the firefighters immediately left the building. Some never got the message to return to the lobby due to the inadequacies of the radio communication system which failed to reach all parts of the building. Others were delayed in leaving because they made the courageous choice to continue assisting people on the upper floors.

Once the second building collapsed it seemed that nothing worse could conceivably occur. The painful truth is that on some deep level I did feel a sense of relief that I was spared from having to give what would have been an excruciating order to have all firefighters leave the building. And I certainly didn't feel good about feeling relieved when so many had just died.

It wasn't until later that night that I was finally assigned to respond downtown. At that point the damage had been done and the long rescue and recovery process began. I organized a group of firefighters and we stopped a city bus for a ride to the Trade Center site. We had all spent our entire careers responding in fire trucks with lights and sirens blaring and very the act of commandeering a normal public transportation vehicle added to the odd tenor of the day.

The bus dropped us off about a half mile from the Trade Center and

I walked down to a staging area a few blocks north of the site to get my assignment. It was very obvious that the staging chief had very been there for the entire day. He was exhausted, covered in dust, and his voice was so hoarse he was barely able to talk. I was assigned to be the sector commander of the northeast portion of the collapse area. None of the things you would normally expect to have were available. I had no respiratory protection, no list of the units I would be supervising, not even a radio to communicate with the odd mix of firefighters, police officers, and civilian volunteers who were climbing all over the mass of twisted steel and debris.

The walk from the staging area to the Trade Center was as odd and surreal as the rest of the day. For blocks and blocks I trudged through ankle-deep gray dust and passed large pieces of metal debris that had randomly scattered throughout lower Manhattan. You could taste the toxic mix of smoke and dust that permeated everything. At one point I noticed a soot-covered office building that I had worked in years before I became a firefighter and for an instant felt a strange, detached sense of a distant chapter in my life.

It was while walking through the middle of all this chaos and devasta-

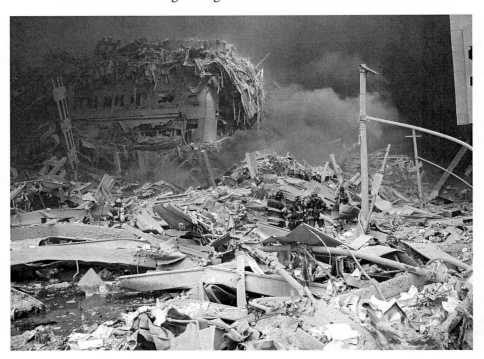

Firefighters working in the devastation of lower Manhattan (photograph by Steve Spak).

tion that I first startied seeing them. Many were lying on the dusty streets, some were still fluttering around in the air. There were hundreds of them. The memos, letters, and legal documents that had been the lifeblood of the everyday work accomplished in those buildings were everywhere, perfectly legible and undamaged, as though some secretary or office manager had just removed them from a printer. It was almost painful to see their pristine state contrasted against the hellish world they had landed in.

I didn't get home until much later that day feeling mentally, physically, and emotionally exhausted. I remember my wife running out of the house in her stocking feet to greet me. She was on the verge of tears. All of our neighbors with "normal" jobs had come home hours before. Although she was accustomed to my disappearing for a regular 24-hour tour by that point I had been gone for 40 tumultuous hours. I sometimes think it's emotionally more difficult to observe a disaster from a distance. Having been immersed in it for so long my feeling was more like "What's the big deal? I'm just tired and want to sleep." I had forced the insanity of the experience out of my mind and my perspective at that point was more in tune with my eight-year-old son who simply asked if soccer tryouts would

Papers from the World Trade Center scattered throughout the streets (photograph by Steve Spak).

be canceled. That being said I certainly know how my wife, and the rest of America, felt on 9/11.

Of the thousands of people who died that day 343 of them were New York City firefighters. Eventually posters with photos of all the people we lost were distributed to firehouses throughout the city. Sometimes, in the course of my workday, I would pause and look at their faces. Some I knew very well. Some I had never met. All are remembered and sorely missed.

Occasionally I still think of the papers, and how those perfectly preserved documents that had once meant so much to so many people lost all their relevance lying in the dust of pulverized Manhattan buildings. And I try so hard to see them as some sort of a metaphor. Of survival, and perspective, and hope for the future.

Mentors and Maniacs

I clearly recall the day I first reported for duty as a brand new probie. It was December and it was cold and the moment I walked into the ancient brick firehouse I was immediately hit by a humid blast of steam heat that mixed with the scents of polished brass, freshly mopped floors, and smoky fire gear. I was "welcomed" by the curious stares of a half dozen men who looked at me in a manner that said, "Who the fuck are you and what are you doing here?" I looked at my new coworkers and they looked at me and the long process of getting to know each other began. That process would go on for 33 years and would introduce hundreds of individuals into my life.

First impressions seemed strongest when I met new people. That was when my image of them was fresh and unaffected by the good or bad things I would learn about them in the future. Without any experience to guide me, my first impressions of new people were totally subjective. And though it may seem rather shallow my initial judgments very often centered on a person's physical appearance. Fairly or not, I made assumptions about them based on how they looked. Were they fat or muscular? Attractive or repulsive? Did their body language project confidence or present a marshmallow-like essence? However, the physical traits soon lost their impact. After spending enough time with someone I no longer noted their crooked teeth, large nose, or bald head. The physical characteristics lost all meaning.

It was the other kind of first impression that remained significant and that was my impression of what their personality might be like. What kind of behavior could I expect from the man sitting across from me on the train? Was he someone to converse with or just another tired and withdrawn commuter? Did the woman I was introduced to at a business meeting (whom I most certainly first evaluated physically) look approachable and open to my ideas or was she closed off and full of herself?

Unspoken but formidable, such evaluations occurred the moment I entered the firehouse. I wondered which of these tough, experienced fire-fighters would become a friend and which would prove to be a foe. They immediately sized me up and, on first glancing at them, I did likewise. My immediate impressions did not all turn out to be accurate. But those first impressions of a room full of firefighters have stayed with me. I remember them all, the old veteran who had seen dozens of new probies over the years and who totally ignored me, the young guy who immediately evaluated me with a critical eye, and the officer who just wanted me to hand him my personnel folder so that he could get started on the tedious additional paperwork my appearance required of him.

And then there was that person I would ultimately most value—the one who showed me the way. Whether or not he was formally given the title, he was the guy who was destined to become my job mentor. I would have a number of mentors over the years and they are the ones who have left the deepest impressions.

Usually the mentor possessed a body of knowledge and experience that I couldn't ever imagine mastering. He approached work every day in a manner that showed it was much more than a just a job to him. It was a role that wasn't limited to any particular rank. The mentors ranged from high-profile chiefs to relatively unknown firefighters. Some were the "mouth" in the kitchen, others were the most subdued. But whoever they were, they generally shared two traits to go along with their impressive experience: they were excited about the job and they were approachable. I worked with these mentors at every rank I held in the New York City Fire Department. Sometimes they actively pursued the role of mentor but often they just set an example with their style.

Dave became my first mentor. Not because he was ordered to, and not even because he choose it. It just kind of happened. Dave was about 50 years old when I first met him. Physically he was a guy who would normally blend into a crowd. He was average height with just the slightest suggestion of a beer gut that reflected his beverage of preference. It was only when I spent some time with him that I saw the depth of his personality. Dave was blessed with a mind as sharp as a tack as well as an ability to appreciate the ridiculousness in life. Though he took the job very seriously he had enough time in the fire department to see right through anything he might consider to be irrelevant nonsense. That included wearing the proper uniform, which had changed numerous times over the course of his career. He would wear whatever type of outfit he happened to retrieve from the back of his locker, and some of them were standard job issue from 15 years prior.

Dave was kind of the poster boy for the old joke about how you can't become a firefighter when you grow up because firefighters never really grow up. He once switched our lieutenant's helmet just before a run came in. The lieutenant was an old, bald-headed guy whose appearance reflected every bit of the 40 years he had put on the job. It was only after operating at a car fire for a half an hour that he realized he was wearing a probie's helmet rather one that identified him as an officer. It was dumb, it was childish, and it was pretty funny to see such a senior man masquerading as a probie.

But that was Dave. Rules meant very little to him. He treated all ranks in the job with an equal amount of humorous disrespect but always in a good-natured manner. To him life was essentially funny and one's prime purpose was to enjoy all aspects of it. He was a great storyteller and would often sit around, beverage in hand, regaling all about his latest escapades. It didn't take me long to really enjoy his company.

There was a serious side of Dave and it often showed in his respect for the work of firefighting. He had seen a lot and knew the dangers of the job. He also knew that there was a right way and a wrong way to do something. The right way would make your job easier and safer, the wrong way could kill you. He was a comedian in the firehouse but on the fireground he became a serious teacher who provided lessons that were always hands-on and practical. After one fire he refused to allow another probie to start packing up the hose until he could show him the errors he had made in the operation. But he always taught in a patient manner that accepted a probie's inexperience without the harsh criticisms that often vented from many of the other, more caustic fire veterans. I caught most of my early jobs with Dave and really benefited from his reassuring presence on the fireground. He was behind me the first time I handled the nozzle at a fire and he guided me through a long and difficult hose stretch up a steep exterior fire escape at my first multiple alarm. And he would always revert back to his easy-going, humorous persona once the fire was over.

Perhaps the thing I liked most about Dave was his immediate acceptance of me as a person. I was very green and inexperienced and required a lot of guidance but to him I was always Tom and not just the latest probie who happen to get assigned to the unit. One night he showed the ultimate sign of acceptance when he offered me a cold beer. Me, a probie, being offered to partake in the communion of alcohol! Drinking was forbidden on the job for everybody and was especially verboten for someone on probation who could easily be fired for infractions during the first year of employment. When I was a probie the department was still transitioning into the modern institution it is today. I had the benefit of learning from the "Babe Ruths" of the fire service, men who had tons of experience and many firefighting lessons to pass on. But along with that experience some of them had habits I could not accept and drinking on the job was one of them. Of course, I declined Dave's offer of the beer but I was actually moved by the fact that he thought enough of me to want to share a brew with me. We were certainly different in age, experience, and temperament but we connected well because of our mutual discomfort with bureaucracy. With Dave the firefighting was everything and the rules be dammed. He would eventually retire and I would move on to other experiences in the job.

Many years later when I became a chief I was sitting in my office reading through the latest department orders and saw Dave's name in the section that recorded the deaths of retired members. I thought of him and the solid firefighting lessons he imparted. And I found myself smiling as I considered the perspective he always maintained. As Dave would have put it, "The job is fire and everything else is bullshit and a person of any rank is capable of screwing up."

A few years after I met Dave I ran into another dinosaur when I was a newly promoted company officer. Sean was a lieutenant and a remnant of the "war years," an era when ghetto firefighters could expect to go to a dozen structural fires each night. Sean was old school both on the job and in his life. He grew up in a gritty Manhattan neighborhood that once had an Irish bar on every corner but had since evolved into a low- income, Hispanic area. And that troubled him on a deep level. Not the most liberal type of guy, he struggled with the changes that were occurring in the city and within the job. But it would be unfair to label Sean as anti-minority. He was more like a walking anachronism who bore the parochial view of his upbringing and that meant that anyone who was not Irish was not to be completely trusted.

He once got a phone call about a routine administrative matter from a battalion chief who happened to be of Italian heritage.

"Lieutenant," the chief said, "that semiannual hydrant inspection re-port is due. Can you get it to me by the end of the tour?"

"Sure, chief, no problem, I'll be sure to finish it up and send it over as soon as I can," Sean responded in a most gracious and friendly manner.

As Sean finished up his conversation with the chief I could hear him say, "OK, chief, you too, chief, have a good day now, hope you have a quiet tour!" followed by a few superfluous "goodbyes" just before he hung up the phone.

But the moment he put down the phone the first thing I heard out of his mouth was "You bald-headed guinea bastard!" Then he turned to me and said, "My father told me never to trust those Italians!"

It wasn't about black or white people, women or Hispanics. No, Sean was truly equal opportunity in outlook. He was unaccepting of *anyone* who happened to be outside his clan. Normally he was usually pretty easy-going but one day he came up to me and looked like he was really upset about something. At the time the department was starting to make sincere efforts at hiring minorities and creating a more diversified workforce. Sean stood right in front of me, his weathered Gaelic countenance bursting with concern, and he sadly blurted out, "This isn't an Irish job anymore!" Of course, firefighting had never been an Irish job but a civil service position that in the past had traditionally attracted the same type of applicant.

Sean had trouble keeping up with the technical innovations on the job as well as the social changes. Eventually computerized mobile data terminals were installed in our trucks to increase response times. They were a great addition but were fairly complex to operate and required some getting used to. Sean's getting-used-to period was rather prolonged. I felt bad for him one time when he was publicly embarrassed over the department radio by an impatient dispatcher. He wasn't quite sure which button he had to push when he was leaving the scene of an incident. I watched as he peered through his reading glasses at the computer screen and desperately hit various function keys while a frustrated dispatcher berated him over the radio.

Sean was old-fashioned, narrow-minded, and resistive to almost any kind of change. And he was probably the best fire officer I ever worked with. Despite his parochial outlook I often observed him stepping up to teach new firefighters regardless of their race or ethnicity. He had seen a lot in his career and well understood the importance of preparing new personnel for the dangers they would face. I sometimes wondered if his Irish obsession was just a part of an ongoing performance in which he portrayed himself in the role of the grumpy old veteran.

Sean had a sense of ease on the fireground that I envied. I really don't think he viewed a fire as a scenario loaded with an endless variety of deadly possibilities, although he was well aware that they existed. To him a fire was more like a place he had been to many times before and was certain to visit again. I shared one of those many visits with him in the Bronx. We were working at a fire in a high-rise apartment building and Sean came in as the officer of the second due engine. The second engine was generally responsible for helping with the hose stretch and then standing by to relieve the first unit when they needed a rest. For a few minutes that allowed Sean to indulge in his favorite pastime—kibitzing. I was very involved in the operation as the first ladder officer but he somehow located me and, with the fire still lapping out the windows, said, "Did you hear what that fuckin' Georgie Boyle said?" referring to a guy we worked with. It was as if we were not working at a fire but chatting over dinner or walking on a golf course. You just can't help but feel a relaxed sense of confidence if you were around a guy like that. It was as if you spent enough time with him some of his vast fireground experience would rub off on you and the luck that carried him safely though decades of dangerous encounters would be passed on. I think I learned as much about command presence from Sean as I did from many of the chiefs I worked with, that sense that no matter how bad things looked we *were* going to put out this fire and things would be OK.

Some mentors were old-school types and some were new school. Eventually the job started to move at a glacially slow pace into the 20th century. The ancient three-ring binders that had been used for decades to run the department were replaced by computers. Training was modernized and PowerPoint was introduced. Colorful graphics and moving bullets replaced the old black-and-white slide presentations that had lulled classrooms full of firefighters to sleep.

As the job gradually morphed into the "new age" FDNY I found myself clinging to the lessons of the old-school teachers but also learned much from the more modern guys. They came on the job with backgrounds that were very different from old-time firefighters. Many of them were well educated and some had left professions as accountants, teachers, or lawyers to become New York City firefighters. They were as comfortable with computers, cell phones, and spread sheets as the traditional veterans had been with plumbing, carpentry, and auto mechanics. While their expertise and style was new, they shared the same passion for the job that the previous generation had. And just being around them added to my professionalism as a company officer and a chief.

Then there were the others. I'm sure you've met them, worked with them, perhaps even live with one of them. While they were vastly outnumbered by those who were willing to help, the "maniacs" always lurked in the background just waiting to disrupt my learning curve. They were to be found at every level in the fire department ranging from firefighter to high-ranking chiefs. And while the personalities varied they shared some common traits. Whether it was cynicism, ego, or downright orneriness that drove them, they had no interest in teaching me and at times seemed to delight in my discomfort. These were generally the firefighters who were mainly interested in getting though 20 years on the job with a minimum of effort and a maximum of complaint. To them the process of setting an example for new personnel was simply not a part of their job description. Sometimes they were "veterans" with all of two years on the job who loved to inflate their identities by inflecting as much pain as possible on the newest probie.

There was a small, select group of chiefs who also managed to fit in the maniac category. You met Phil Crusoe in a previous chapter. He was an upper-echelon chief who considered intimidation a major part of his job description (why bother to mentor when your position allows you to continually harass and micromanage?). I actually learned a lot by watching him in action since he was a shining example of how *not* to lead people. Blessed with the power to intimidate and annoy he provided a case study in bad management.

The majority of chiefs I worked for were decent, hardworking people. But an institution that promoted from within sometimes led to a very myopic management perspective that left me shaking my head in frustration. When I was a deputy chief I had to send an immediate report to headquarters when a civilian was killed or seriously injured at a fire. It was a two-page outline specifying minute details about the victim and the fire operation. I once forwarded one of these reports for a person who had suffered smoke inhalation and was being treated at a hospital. The chief who was my superior for that tour tended to go through these things with a fine-tooth comb and would accept nothing short of an absolutely perfect report. He immediately got back to me and complained that I had not filled out the "cause of death" section of the form. I patiently explained to him that the injured person was in fact still alive to which he responded a brief "Oh." I wanted to offer to drive over to the hospital and personally kill the victim so that the report could be both complete and perfect but he probably would not have appreciated, or perhaps even recognized, the sarcasm. And besides, that just wasn't my style. Fortunately, I also had the opportunity to work for many excellent chiefs whose leadership and style I did try to emulate.

I worked with them both—the mentors and the maniacs. And while it was definitely a much better experience being with the former, I drew a great deal from both. One group taught me the route to take and one showed the way to avoid. The really difficult individuals may have had more of an immediate impact because of the frustration they caused, but in the long run it was the more subtle professionalism of the positive mentors that I retained and was shaped by.

Time flies by in any profession. Before you know it you have five or 10 or 20 years of experience to mold you into a competent individual and, just possibly, a mentor to someone else. Not long before I retired I received a letter from a very solid officer who had worked for me and had just been promoted. In the letter he thanked me for what he felt was the good example I had set for him. I was surprised, and very pleased, that I had unknowingly assumed some part of that mentor role that had always been provided for me. I guess the student ultimately becomes the teacher whether he plans it or not.

In the fire service, as in life, you leave a footprint wherever you tread. I hope that my tracks were as deep as the ones that others had left for me.

My Two Worlds

It was as though I had two separate identities. I was the guy who lived in a safe, quiet suburb, shopped at the mall, and occasionally popped up at the town library or kids' soccer game. But I was also the person who would periodically disappear for 24 hours to assume a completely different role in a maelstrom of urban noise and chaos. And even as I was relaxing in the comfort of home I was often thinking about what might occur when I returned to my other world. What inevitable disaster awaited to test me and challenge my ability to keep myself and others alive? Would my skills and experience once again be sufficient to safely manage it all or would the next tour be the one where I finally slipped and, in a moment of poor judgment, caused someone to get hurt?

Whenever I found myself thinking too much like that I would force myself to stop. A vivid imagination is not your ally if your vocation involves a constant confrontation with death and destruction. If you thought too much about the negative possibilities in life you probably wouldn't be able to get out of bed in the morning, much less go to work. Nonetheless, the repressed fears and doubts were ever-present.

I was always a great believer in the power of using routine as an antidote to the pressures of a stressful job. And those routines would begin long before I even arrived at the firehouse. Just before I got into my car to drive to work I would pause for a moment and look up at the very tops of the tall, swaying pine trees on my property. It served a practical purpose since the motion of the trees gave a clear indication of both the direction and intensity of the wind: a factor that might influence my firefighting strategy during the tour. But I think the routine may have had even deeper roots than that. Watching the clouds pass beyond the gently dancing tree limbs provided one last deep breath of home, beauty, and comfort before heading to the city.

The commute itself was a routine. I would generally leave around the same time in the late afternoon and follow the same route. Usually I would stop at a traffic light just before getting on the highway. While waiting for the light to change I would stare at a small pond that sat on the right side of the road and watch as the silent wake of a lone duck rippled across the surface. Often it was at that precise moment that it would hit me. At that very instant there were men, women, or children walking around in New York City oblivious to the certainty that in a few hours their lives would be forever changed. While that duck gently glided across the pond someone was going to be maimed or killed by a fire, an accident, or some other trauma.

I am one of thousands who grew up and lived in the city before finding my bucolic escape in suburbia. Fire became a part of my urban memory. I learned as a child that smoke is not just a visual element, but a component that gets embedded in your senses. My brother and I watched fires from our tenement window in Brooklyn. The smoke that drifted in had a flavor that was both exotic and frightening. My father fought fires for 30 years in the city and came home from work with that scent on his body. Years later my wife would discover that repeated washing could not eliminate that same scent from me.

Despite my background, I was always amazed at the number of fires and emergencies that occurred each day in the city. The fire department radio spewed out an endless litany of human loss and suffering. A car crashed in Queens and passengers were trapped. CPR was in progress in mid–Manhattan. Two floors of a tenement were burning in the Bronx.

How many broken bodies did I see through the years? How many family photos and children's toys lay soaked and ruined? Each of the deaths reaffirmed my appreciation of life, but you don't just shake off 33 years of destructive images. Nor do you forget the gems of human dignity you also observe. You see it in the person who loses everything he has in a fire but takes the time to thank you for extinguishing it. And you see it in the determined faces of filthy, exhausted firefighters sifting through 9/11 rubble.

So what was the Holy Grail that drew me to this career? Was it as simple as a desire to experience some real excitement in an otherwise predictable life? Maybe I was afraid of falling into some corporate rut and needed to do something really unusual and challenging. Or perhaps I was seeking an identity, as if the job title of "firefighter" magically bestowed on a person some special attributes whether they were deserved or not. Some psychologist might even view it as an effort at connecting with my father. Most likely it was a combination of a lot of things. But whatever the reasons I know that the experience had profound effects on me. In a strange way, I still miss the heart-thumping responses to Bronx and Manhattan fires now that I am retired from that line of work. For that world has forever become a part of my psyche.

Forests, deer, and wide-open soccer fields will all be a part of my children's memories. Fires, building collapses and squalid tenements will not. For this I am thankful. But I sometimes wonder if the "dual citizenship" I felt from being immersed in both of these worlds somehow kept me from being totally comfortable residing in either.

I would drive past the pond again when I returned home from a 24-hour work shift in the city. I remember how clean the air tasted when I rolled down the car window and used to be amazed that 45 minutes of driving could change so much. As the environment changed, so did my identity and I would reclaim those parts of myself that I had to put on hold to fulfill the role of an urban fire chief. Nothing in the pond had changed in the time I had been gone. But once again, in some subtle but deep way, I had.

Later, in the comfort of my living room, I could sometimes catch the scent of wood burning in a neighbor's fireplace, a scent that transported me back to that world I often left but never fully escaped.

Let It Burn

I often came home from work bearing a sense of accomplishment along with that inevitable essence of smoke on my body. It was a good feeling to know that I had a part in extinguishing a difficult fire or handling a building collapse or resolving some other kind of disaster. When things went well it felt like there were very few challenges that the FDNY couldn't manage. That was certainly true for all of the "normal" emergency operations in New York City which were generally settled quickly and safely. New Yorkers may have had their doubts about how the city was governed or felt alienated by political manipulations in Washington, D.C., but for the most part they liked the fire department. That was a government agency that got things done. The fire department actually came quickly when there was trouble and accomplished its work in a totally apolitical manner.

In a sense our work involved wrestling with the forces of nature: the smoke, heat, fire, and toxic materials that were constantly being generated at incidents throughout a large and congested city. Always, it seemed, we came out on top in that contest. But of course, nature expresses its power in more ways than one and whether that strength is reflected through a fire, volcano, or solar eclipse, the message is clear. Mother Nature will not be messed with nor will she allow you any delusions about overcoming her.

Hurricane Sandy rolled up the East Coast in October 2012 destroying beaches, buildings, entire communities, and any illusions we may have harbored about the level of our ability to confront natural disaster. I seemed to have had a knack for being on duty when hurricanes hit New York City. In the previous year I had worked through Hurricane Irene and experienced a busy tour involving damaged buildings and numerous downed tree limbs in my response area. But overall it had not been that bad considering what was to follow in 2012. For most of us Sandy redefined our concept of what a hurricane was and the effects it could have. But it certainly didn't sneak up on us. The weather service had predicted the storm's expected path and potential danger. I sat at home and nervously watched their dire predictions throughout the afternoon before I left for work. Of course, going to work also meant leaving my family to face the storm alone for a long period, a scenario that just added to the stress.

I prepared my home as well as I could by putting fresh batteries in flashlights, securing windows, and even setting screws in precut sheets of plyboard so they could be rapidly secured over any broken windows. However, no matter how much I did I couldn't help but feel that I was abandoning my family to unknown dangers and I had an image of my wife desperately struggling with pieces of plywood as the wind whipped through shattered windows. I knew I had to go to work but felt torn between my responsibilities for both the job and my family. Getting my home ready for the hurricane's assault was similar to supervising a fire operation. I could plan and prepare for problems on the fireground but I couldn't actually do the work myself. If my family was going to be endangered by the storm I wasn't even going to be there. They were going to have to cope for themselves.

I drove to work that afternoon plagued with a sense of dread for what might happen over the next 24 hours both at home and in the city. The moment I walked through the door of the firehouse I sensed that there was a different atmosphere in the place. There were more people than normal milling about since additional firefighters had been held over for the storm. Chain saws, generators, and gas cans were lined up on the apparatus floor all primed and ready for the coming assault. When I walked upstairs to my office there were stacks of correspondence piled on my desk outlining emergency procedures that were going to be implemented for the duration of the storm. Maps of the city were tacked up to the walls highlighting areas that were prone to flooding. It kind of reminded me of all the nerve-wracking preparations for the D-Day invasion I had read about in history books. I wasn't going to invade a country but it was clear that something big was about to attack us.

I began to tackle the mountain of administrative work that had accumulated and quickly fell into a routine that seemed to insulate me from the wind and rain that swept through the city in advance of the hurricane. The rattling of the windows was regularly drowned out by the constantly ringing office phones, each call informing us of new problems that had to be addressed. An engine company was having mechanical problems with their apparatus, the oil tanks were getting low in one of the fuel depots, and one of our major intersections was starting to flood. On top of all this there were citywide telephone conferences scheduled to be held about every two hours throughout the night. It was shaping up to be one of those taxing, sleepless nights that showed no more sign of letting up than did the storm. When, about five hours into the tour, a run finally came in I was ready to escape from the office mania and get out to actually fight a fire.

It looked like it was going to be a good job. The first due engine reported that heavy fire was pushing through the roof of a restaurant out on City Island and a second alarm had been quickly transmitted. Normally that would have been a significant challenge in itself and as I responded I tried to imagine how the weather conditions might make it even more difficult. Both the rain and wind had picked up substantially since the start of the tour.

City Island is a tiny, remote community just off the eastern edge of the Bronx. Once you drive over the small bridge that leads there you find yourself in a world completely unlike the rest of the borough. Less than two miles long and barely a half mile wide it resembles a tiny New England sea coast town more than a New York City neighborhood. It was if Walt Disney had visited the Bronx and was so scared by the rest of the place that he decided to create a "Sea Shore Land" to escape to. Boat yards and restaurants line the one main street that runs the length of the island and you often see people enjoying picnics and fishing right off of the bridge. Accustomed as I was to the rest of the city, I always sort of felt like I was on a mini-vacation whenever I went out there, especially when the weather was nice.

Tonight the weather was certainly not very nice. It took some time to get there and once we arrived we had to park several blocks away from the fire since numerous emergency vehicles had already lined up on the main road. I did a quick size-up as I walked down toward the fire and things were actually looking pretty good. The burning restaurant was the very last building on the island and was surrounded only by trees and waterfront. That meant that the fire was unlikely to spread to other structures even though it was burning intensely. A couple of tower ladders were already pouring heavy-caliber streams of water on to the building, one from a position at the end of the main road and one from a side street. All in all, it looked very much like a typical "surround and drown" operation that would take some time to complete but would eventually extinguish the fire with minimal risk to the firefighters. In the street I met up with the staff chief assigned for the tour who had also responded to the scene. He was a solid, experienced guy I always enjoyed working with. After discussing the operation we both kind of figured that there wouldn't be too many key strategic changes needed, just patience and a willingness to deal with the weather conditions.

A few minutes later the officer assigned to one of the tower ladders came up to me. His rig was set up and operating from a position on the main street about 70 feet from the water's edge. He indicated that the water had risen a few feet since they had started to work and, thinking that we may have to reposition his apparatus, I told him to get his men ready to move the truck further away from the end of the dock. I figured that as the tide rose we would continue the attack on the fire from a safer position. When I mentioned this development to the staff chief I was totally unprepared for his response. He immediately ordered all units to shut down their water streams and prepare to leave the island. Quickly, decisively, and somewhat surprisingly we were abandoning the operation altogether. When I relayed the order to the units they were equally shocked. This was not in the department's DNA. The FDNY didn't just shut down and run away.

In retrospect the staff chief's decision made perfect sense. These were not normal conditions. Hurricane Sandy had changed the rules of the game. The chief realized that he had numerous units operating at a fire in a building that was isolated at the end of an island and was not threatening any nearby structures. Those fire units were also in an isolated position. They were all parked at the end of an island that had just one small bridge as a means of escape and the storm was bringing excessive winds and a rapidly rising tide. Lingering too long at a fire that was not going to threaten the neighborhood meant risking the possibility of trapping a substantial number of men and equipment on the island for the duration of the storm. That could prove to be catastrophic since those resources were likely to be needed in other parts of the city later on. Staff chiefs were accustomed to maintaining a big picture view of overall department needs, a skill that was sometimes lost on those of us who were more geared to viewing and attacking the immediate and local fire challenges we normally dealt with.

Still, I did feel really strange as we drove away from the fire. Staring back through the haze and driving rain I could still see the building burning away. It was just sitting there with flames shooting through the roof, oblivious to the storm, and to us, and showing no sign that the fire department had ever even been there. In the past I had fought numerous fires. Many of them were enormously destructive and a few of them were of historical significance. But I had never left a fire. As I looked back I wondered if this was the first time in the entire history of the FDNY that this had ever happened.

The rest of the night was a very quiet one for me. I had no other incidents and just continued to monitor the storm and perform the needed administrative duties. It was as if the Bronx was, once again, not only the city's poorest borough but also its most forgotten borough. Even Mother Nature seemed to ignore it as the hurricane proceeded to wreak havoc on

A typical "surround-and-drown" operation. Only once did I ever just walk away from a building that was still burning like this (photograph by Bill Tompkins).

the Rockaways and flood major sections of Manhattan. I had survived the storm and, with the exception of some scary moments and minor house damage, my family was OK at home.

I could still catch glimpses of that burning restaurant as we drove away from City Island. What I couldn't know at the time was that in just a few short years I'd be looking back at my entire career through the rear-view mirror.

Leaving the Tribe

Before I joined the FDNY I had a hard time actually seeing myself doing that type of work. My father had been on the job for many years but the fire department was a radical departure from the work world I had anticipated being in. It was not the typical path that my education normally led to. But when I finally left the job after 33 years of firefighting I felt just the opposite. It was difficult for me to envision myself without it. I was not just leaving a job, I was also abandoning a lifestyle as well as an important part of my identity. It wasn't as if there would be another comparable position for me to slide into. I had worked in a somewhat esoteric field and was not about to hook up with a similar position in a bank or law firm. What I had done over the years was just not going to be replaced by a related job.

I felt what a professional athlete must feel when he retires. I fully appreciated all of the great experiences and I was certainly relieved to have survived such a career in reasonably good shape. I was also looking forward to the luxury of more free time without having to use a portion of that time to recuperate from the physical and mental assaults of the job. But there was a definite sense of loss. I realized that nothing I would ever do with the rest of my life would provide quite the same level of stimulation. I was moving away from my role of supervising large groups of men and using millions of dollars' worth of equipment to combat fires and resolve intense, life-and-death scenarios. Instead, I would be writing and lecturing and enjoying time with my family and taking out the garbage on Thursday, all of which were great things but at the same time seemed rather tame and predictable matters compared to what I had been doing as a firefighter. I knew that on some deep level I would miss the chaos of the job. The stress of the work also provided the inspiration of the work. It is possible to get addicted to experiences that are laced with adrenaline.

I found it difficult to share such feelings with people who had not worked under similar circumstances. One time I had a conversation with a man who had spent his life working in "professional" office environments.

He was a decent, intelligent person but when I tried to describe the gruff, aggressive nature of firehouse life and the stresses of fighting a fire he responded by saying that he knew exactly what I was talking about because he worked with computer programmers and his work world was just like that. Now I've got all the respect in the world for computer programmers but as I pictured a bunch of guys in pressed shirts and ties sitting in front of computer screens I knew that he had absolutely no idea what I was talking about and rather than pursuing it I just changed the topic of our conversation.

People were usually impressed when they knew that I had been a firefighter and would sometimes say things like "Thank you for your service" (and I would think, "What 'service'?" I accomplished some good things but it was a job that I probably did more for my own fulfillment rather than any lofty humanitarian reasons). However, it seemed like only a firefighter really knew what I was talking about when I would relive one of my fireground experiences or when I spoke about those aspects of the job that I really missed. I quickly realized that an important part of retiring from firefighting would be accepting the challenge of forging a new sense of identity that was separate from the ready-made one that my work had provided.

At first I was reluctant to tell people that I was retired and I hated the "Ret." abbreviation that I had to put after the "Thomas Dunne, Deputy Chief" handle that appeared on my resume. When I lectured to a group of people at a convention and was introduced as a fire safety expert and an ex–FDNY chief I would concentrate on the "ex" part of my title. To me it was a painful reminder of my new status as if to say I was over the hill, a professional dinosaur. Initially I felt like my expertise and experience was overshadowed by the fact that I was no longer a chief or a firefighter. Although I had seen and done a lot it was all in the past and seemingly gone forever. I could relate some good stories and teach some important lessons but the glaring fact was that I was no longer actually doing the work. I could no longer refer to the lessons that were highlighted at the fire I had just a few days ago like I had done when I lectured as an active firefighter.

As I moved on from the job the job also moved on from me. Just as it does in every aspect of life, time changes things. I was always cordially welcomed back when I would spend time with people I used to work with. But now there was a clear delineation between their world and mine. We could share memories of difficult fires we had fought or reminisce about some hilarious moments we shared in the sanctity of the firehouse kitchen (the image of the flying plate of chicken parmesan that killed the mouse will always be one of the indelible highlights of my career) but they were still doing the work and I was not, a reality which created an inherent separateness. I had not been to the fire that they had the night before. I had not worked with that obnoxious new officer who had just transferred into the division nor had I read about that upsetting new regulation or procedure that had just been introduced on the latest department order. Invariability there were also the new faces, the young firefighters who had been hired since I retired and with whom I had shared no past experiences. We would be introduced and they would look at me in a respectful but awkward manner, no doubt wondering, "Who the hell is this old guy?" while I would return their gaze and think, "Boy, does this kid have a lot to learn." Just two ships passing each other at the opposite ends of our careers.

When I was a firefighter I would often see retired guys come to visit the firehouse. Some had recently left the job and everyone seemed to have shared work experiences with them. Others had been retired for years and very few of the current firefighters even knew who they were. You could instantly tell how they were handling retirement. Most looked really happy and would speak enthusiastically about their families or the projects they were involved in or the trips they had taken. They gave visual evidence to the fact that there was indeed life after the fire department. But some looked rather lost, like they had left their best days on the job and had been unable to replace them with new experiences. They would often come in with a well-intended box of doughnuts that they would share with anyone who joined them in the kitchen. And eventually, as the on duty guys moved on to any required chores or simply to more relevant conversations with people they were actually working with, they would slowly leave the firehouse to go wherever it was they were spending their time, certain to be coming back again for another visit before too long.

I thought those guys were really good people but couldn't help but see them as kind of sad. They seemed like they were still emotionally stuck in a job that they could no longer be a part of, a job that had grown away from them. They were kind of like that box of doughnuts. When the pastries were fresh people would come to the table to eat and converse. After a while the ones that weren't eaten would get stale and just sit there. And eventually the remnants would be thrown out, discarded and forgotten, when the kitchen was being cleaned.

As much as I knew I was going to miss the job I knew that I would never become one of the doughnut guys. My fire department roots ran as deep as anyone's. A job that I had originally intended to be a one-year, in-and-out experience had morphed into a 33-year career. I did love the job but even as I was doing it I didn't want to feel like my entire world was encompassed by it. I kept parts of my life, and parts of myself, separate from it. And while that alienated me from certain aspects of fire department culture it also allowed me to stay true to myself and ultimately proved to be a key factor in helping me move on from the job. The fire department was a big part of my life but my life was bigger than the fire department.

Still, I was somewhat surprised by how well I transitioned into my next chapter in life. I took a lot of pride in the things I had done in the FDNY and those experiences left me with a quiet sense of confidence that wasn't there before I had been a firefighter. I discovered that the knowledge I had accumulated translated well into teaching others and there were lessons I could offer to both the firefighting and civilian communities. I may have missed the excitement of the work but I retained the awareness it imparted and wanted to share it with others.

There was something else that helped me in my transition, a factor that had been on my mind for some time. And that had to do with luck. I knew all too well that I had been incredibly lucky in a very dangerous profession for a very long time. I had an image of luck as a full glass of wine. We were all allotted a certain amount of it to begin with and then it would slowly be used up over time. I personally knew a few really good guys who stayed on the job too long only to have their excellent careers end with a disastrous fire or some other catastrophic experience. As I responded to fires toward the end of my career on some level I couldn't help but think if I was going to the one where I would make a mistake on the fireground that would hurt my men or if this was the incident that had factors beyond my control that would lead to a disaster I could never live down. My love/hate relationship with the excitement of the fireground went on until I went to my last fire. Thankfully, when I left there was still some wine in my glass.

At night I find that I still have dreams about the job. Sometimes they can be very frightening and I will find myself trying to escape from some unseen danger or desperately attempting to find my way out of a smoke-filled maze. More often they reflect the challenging realities of commanding a fire and I dream that I am unable to communicate with someone to relay some vital information or I am ordering men to perform tactics that just don't seem to get accomplished. The dreams, like the reality, can be upsetting and frustrating experiences. But now they are not my reality, just images of what might have been.

In the short time that I've been retired I find that I am just as busy as I was when I was on the job. I miss the FDNY but each day seems to bring additional projects to take on, more lecture opportunities, and brand new avenues to explore. Still, I occasionally look back on it all. I had the pleasure of doing a job for many years that I really enjoyed. And over that time I grew with the job. When I started I was single, somewhat naïve, and hadn't experienced some of life's most significant events. When I left I was married, had children, and through the job I had met an amazing variety of people and witnessed unforgettable sights. The work left me with a lot of positive things.

It also left me with one unanswerable question.

Why Me?

It was late July and I was working in Manhattan when I got a phone call from a friend. He was a chief in a nearby battalion and our paths had crossed numerous times over the years. We had both worked in the Bronx where we had fought a number of fires together. Periodically we would touch base with each other and gossip and about the rumors and petty annoyances that inevitably surfaced in any large organization. Our conversation quickly got on the topic of the Father's Day fire, a tragedy that had occurred in June and was still fresh in the minds of everyone in the department. At that incident an explosion had suddenly started a fire in a hardware store, killing three firefighters and injuring many others. I had not been to the operation but witnessed some of the effects when I went to the hospital on the Upper East Side of Manhattan where several of the injured men were transported and some of their visibly distraught family members had already gathered.

This was the type of tragedy that every chief feared and did all he could to keep from happening. But despite all our best efforts sometimes there were factors at play that were beyond anyone's control. It was as if fate had intervened. Something my friend said to me in our conversation will always echo in my mind. "Tommy," he said, "there but for the grace of God go you or I." We both realized that at another time, at another operation, any of us could be the unfortunate ones.

That was the last time I ever spoke to him. About six weeks later he was one of the thousands who were killed on 9/11. Fate, or the grace of God, or whatever it is that runs the universe determined that his life was to end, abruptly, and without any sense of logic or reason.

I've always been kind of fascinated by the parallel universes we live in. At the same time the bomb was dropped on Hiroshima in 1945 a group of kids were enjoying a baseball game somewhere in Kansas. At the precise moment those planes hit the World Trade Center towers on 9/11 someone was enjoying a cup of coffee in Monhegan Island, Maine, another person was casually reading the morning newspaper in Cozad, Nebraska, and several people in Los Angeles were just getting out of bed, oblivious to the shocking events that were unfolding on the East Coast. So much horrific stuff can happen in one place while at the same time, in another location, all is peaceful. There is no right or wrong to this, it's just the way it is.

Not long ago, while I was sleeping in the comfort of my home, a firefighter was dying in the Bronx, a mere 45-minute drive from where I live. I am affected by every death that occurs in the FDNY but I found this one to be especially difficult to think about. Certainly it was hard to see that he was young and married and had small children. But it hit me even more because he was killed by a freak accident that occurred in the same area, and on the same streets, that I had worked in for many years doing the exact same job. This was also the first line of duty death that occurred since I retired. The tragedy reinforced the fact that the job, and all of its dangers, was now behind me. I survived and this man did not and I continue to enjoy my family, to write my book, and to live my life while his family must go through emotional agony.

What is the driving force behind the circumstances that determine our fates? How can just one phone call, or the difference of a few feet, or the decision to turn left instead of right become so decisive in creating a chain of events that can have such overwhelming effects?

I cannot even to begin to fathom how or, of more relevance, why I came out on the positive side of a parallel universe. Why have I been given the opportunity to retire and continue to explore and enjoy myriad good experiences in life while others were not? I didn't do anything special to earn such a blessing. It's not as if I was a better firefighter or a more capable chief. Those who did not survive performed the job just as well as I did if not better. And they may well have been kinder and more giving persons than I ever was.

I have no strong philosophical or religious beliefs to guide me in such musings. But I do feel obligated to make full use of the gifts that I have been given. I have the physical and emotional nicks and dents that must be expected from doing the work I chose for to do for so many years but I also have a good life and a supporting family and a pension to sustain both. I enjoy and appreciate all of it but I just can't shed the image of those left behind who were not as lucky.

Survival, it seems, comes with servings of both joy and guilt.

Final Thoughts

It is, no doubt, my earliest conscious memory. I am standing in a small bedroom in a Brooklyn row frame tenement. My mother and father are there and they are looking at an old, white-haired man who is sleeping on the bed. Nothing is being said but I'm vaguely aware that something very significant is happening. I am not sure who the man is but I can sense that there is some sort of connection between him and my parents. The room seems very somber and quiet and the only noise I hear is the incessant ticking of an alarm clock that sits on a side table.

The man was, I'm sure, my grandfather who died when I was a very young child and of whom I have no other memories. I was far too little to recognize the imagery of that clock or to realize that, for the first time in my short existence, I was being confronted with existential issues of life, death, and transition.

I don't know what my grandfather may have imagined in his dream state or what he recalled in conscious moments. I do hope that he retained happy memories as he laid there sick and dying. When I look back on the scene I don't remember much of him but I clearly remember the clock and wonder where his thoughts drifted as he looked at life from the tail end of his allotted time. Was he content with what he had accomplished? Were there any regrets about things he did or longings for experiences he was denied?

The career choice I pursued has made it much easier to put such things into perspective. My experiences on the fireground have certainly highlighted the reality that we are all constantly balancing on the precipice of destruction and mortality. But in a strange way that awareness has left me with a far more positive outlook on life. It's as if a long immersion into disaster has deepened my appreciation of all the beautiful and peaceful moments that also exist in life. And the knowledge that the proverbial clock is always ticking only reinforces the value of the here and now. I try to keep that in mind whenever I face the petty annoyances of life. And I carry that perspective with me as I perform the routine chores of life. If I drive into town to pick up groceries or go the hardware store or return a book to the library, it's never sufficient for me to just handle the errands. I also have to take a few moments to savor the changing color of the leaves on the trees or pause to watch the ripples in the stream that flows so serenely through the town or even sit in a trendy café to enjoy a leisurely cup of fashionably overpriced coffee.

Which moments in my life will seem of most importance when I am looking back? I do hope there is no ticking clock when I am reminiscing, for that is a sound I find most annoying and much prefer the cool, silent efficiency of a digital clock. Having said that I will, of course, remember the people in my life, especially those I loved. And what it was like to be at the actual beginning of life as I held both of my children when they were just seconds old. I will also recall how it felt to ski down a mountain and to swim in the ocean, the comfort of wearing worn denim, and the fragrant scent of a freshly cut piece of pine.

But I think I will also recall the fires and the chaotic scenes in the middle of the night where men yelled and windows shattered and urgent messages screeched out of the fireground radios. And the strange beauty of the flames as they lit up the sky and roared through the dark, muted city, so primal, powerful, and destructive.

That too I will remember.

Index

Numbers in **bold italics** indicate pages with illustrations

199